W9-ACC-304

TOKYO FASHION

A Comic Book

Nodoka

Getting Started

Do you have mornings where you think, "I have no time to worry about my clothes. Even if I did, I'd rather spend that time thinking about other things"? The best days are the ones when you spend no time picking out your clothes and still end up looking very fashionable and stylish.

On days when I don't have a lot of time, I end up going into a downward spiral. First, I can't find anything to match the skirt I want to wear, and then I start complaining about how nothing I own looks any good. In the end, I get disappointed in myself, thinking that maybe I just don't have any fashion sense. Is it just me? Don't you think that's a huge waste of time?

What does being "fashionable" mean, anyway? Generally, being fashionable takes attention to detail and willpower.

There are so many fashion rules to follow.

"Of course, you can't let people see your thermal wear."
"It's chic to show off your ankles, even in the winter!"
"The higher the heel, the better!"

It's overwhelming to think that if I don't follow all these rules in my daily life, I won't look fashionable.

I don't have the **time**, **willpower** or **money** to be fashionable like that!

But if I only wear simple, safe designs and no flashy patterns so that other people don't think I look strange, I won't enjoy myself.

I've been trying to find a solution to this for ages. There has to be a way to wear clothing that I'll enjoy and feel comfortable in, but that will also look stylish.

In this book, I'll reveal the results of my research: simple rules for looking fashionable. If you follow these rules, you'll definitely look stylish and sophisticated.

"Buy a striped shirt."
"You don't need to try clothes on."
"Try wearing a watch."

These are the sorts of suggestions I'll be providing; suggestions that can be quickly implemented just by buying something. I won't be including chapters about obvious things like being careful about wearing leggings or anything like that. My goal is to make sure you look as good as possible for as little money as possible. Use that leftover money on something else!

To make it as easy to understand, I'll use a bunch of comics to explain things.

In addition, I'm including the best way to coordinate outfits with men and other family members. Please feel free to use it to choose clothing for your loved ones. Nothing could make me happier than knowing that people out there are putting this book to good use.

NODOKA, A WOMAN AROUND 40, WHO LIKES TO **SEEM** FASHIONABLE. A LAZY, SLOBBY SORT.

MINYAKO, THE CAT WHO FREELOADS AT NODOKA'S HOUSE. SHE CAN TALK. SHE'S HAD A LONG LIFE, SO SHE'S GOT A WIDE BREADTH OF KNOWLEDGE.

CONTENTS

Part 1: FOR WOMEN

How to look stylish when you've got zero time to think about it!

////// Tip # **1** //////

Part 2: FOR MEN

It's pretty easy to look fashionable if you're a man.

Part 1

FOR WOMEN

REMEMBER TO PAIR DENIM
WITH GLAMOROUS CLOTHING.

*How to look stylish when you've
got zero time to think about it!*

01 How to look amazing just by putting on a watch in the morning.

PLAID PANTS ARE A LITTLE OLD-MANNISH, BUT IF YOU PAIR THEM WITH A FEMININE CHIFFON BLOUSE, YOU WILL GET A SWEET AND SALTY MIX THAT IS WELL-BALANCED!

I RECOMMEND WEARING A MEN'S WRISTWATCH WHEN YOU'RE AT WORK. YOU'LL LOOK VERY SHARP, AND YOU'LL BE ABLE TO CHECK THE TIME MUCH MORE EASILY THANKS TO THE LARGE SIZE OF THE WATCH FACE.

MATCHING THE COLOR OF YOUR SHOES TO YOUR WATCHBAND GIVES YOU AN AIR OF EFFORTLESS CHIC.

- Fast fashion striped chiffon blouse
- Plaid ankle-cropped stretch pants
- Tan pumps
- Black-and-navy tote

Hey, do you wear a wristwatch? I bet that since you can check the time on your cell phone, you haven't felt the need to wear one for some time. However, the subtle gesture of a woman checking her watch is incredibly cool.

A wristwatch is an easy item to help you look amazing during the day.

With a delicate women's watch, you can draw attention to yourself.

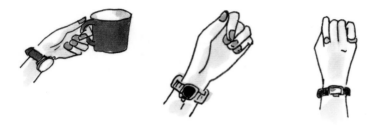

A men's watch makes you look cool and smooth.

Even if you're not all that interested in using a watch, give it a try as a bracelet instead. If you wear a silver or gold watch, it imparts a glow to your hand that really makes you shine.

I recommend watches with simple faces that are white or black.

Use a digital watch with your fancy or minimalist outfits. It becomes an accent piece.

When you're wearing a casual look with a t-shirt and denim, be careful of wearing a digital watch because it might make you look like an elementary school boy.

02 Make your tops simple and your bottoms flashy.

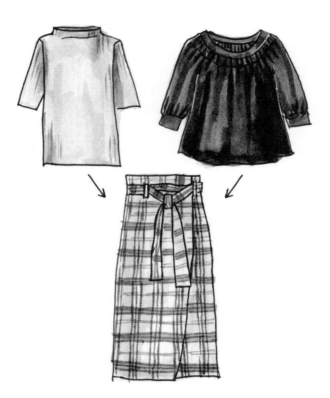

- Soft cotton gathered blouse, black
- Ribbed high-neck tee, gray
- Tie-back plaid skirt

There are easy ways to make sure your outfit is fashionable. One of them is to wear flashy bottoms with a top with a simple color.

Make your top beige, white, black or another basic color. They'll match whatever bottom you pair them with, so you don't need to spend any time worrying over it.

Basic colors are important, but the patterns and designs don't have to be simple.

If you want to wear a flashy top, make sure that you match it with more simple, plain-colored bottoms.

When you wear a chiffon skirt, changing the top can change the feel of the whole outfit.

MATCH A THIN SWEATER WITH ANY BOTTOM AND YOU'LL GET A GREAT MINIMALIST LOOK.

FOR A CASUAL DAY, JUST MATCH IT WITH A PLAIN TEE, SNEAKERS AND A BALLCAP.

A TOTE WITH BLACK STITCHING IS REALLY SOPHISTICATED!

- Ribbed V-neck black drape sweater
- High-waisted chiffon pleated skirt Sandals
- Beige tote bag

- Cotton twill cap
- Crew neck gray tee
- High-waisted chiffon pleated skirt
- Canvas sneakers
- Black circle crossbody bag

You can use the same tops to make new outfits with different pants.

IF YOU PURCHASE TOPS IN BASIC COLORS AND SHOP FOR COLOR POPS AMONG THE 12 COLORS FOUND IN A SET OF COLORED PENCILS, DRESSING WILL BE A LOT EASIER.

THE PLAIN T-SHIRT FROM THE PREVIOUS ILLUSTRATION AND THE THIN SWEATER CAN MATCH EITHER ONE OF THE PICTURED BOTTOMS.

- Crew neck gray tee
- High-waisted green chinos
- Ribbed V-neck black drape sweater
- High-rise cigarette jeans

03

Wear frills and ribbons with khaki pants and instantly look incredibly stylish.

MIXING KHAKI OUTERWEAR WITH A MINIMALIST OUTFIT LETS YOU WEAR YOUR BRAND-NAME ITEMS CASUALLY.

FOR A WORK OUTFIT, MATCH THIS BREEZY SKIRT WITH A TAILORED TOP! IT LOOKS VERY NEAT AND TIDY.

- Nylon khaki trench coat
- Navy V-neck tee
- White circular skirt
- Black heels

"The only thing that doesn't match khaki is khaki," they say. This means that any other color goes well with khaki, making it an all-purpose color.

However, wearing khaki makes your outfit lean a little more towards a casual look. When wearing khaki, if you pair things like ribbons and frills, which may normally be unsuited to you, the khaki will help them work well as part of a classy adult outfit.

Lavender and Khaki

LAVENDER AND KHAKI—A COLOR COMBO I'D LOVE TO SEE PEOPLE TRY!! THE MELLOW IMAGE OF LAVENDER WITH MACHO KHAKI GIVES YOU HIGH FASHION POINTS.

A BASKET PURSE WITH BLACK ACCENTS MEANS THAT EVEN THOUGH IT'S MADE OF WOVEN STRAW, IT DOESN'T GIVE OFF TOO HOMEY A VIBE.

IT'S NOT A COLOR COMBO YOU SEE ALL THAT MUCH, BUT THE COMPATIBILITY IS SO GOOD THAT YOU'D STAND OUT JUST FOR THAT.

- Wide khaki chino pants
- Sandals
- Basket purse with black ribbon accents

Pink and Khaki

A BUTTERFLY BOW WITH SMALL LOOPS LOOKS SOPHISTICATED.

PINK AND KHAKI—IF YOU WANT TO WEAR PINK, GO TO KHAKI FIRST!!

CHOOSE NARROW-LEGGED KHAKI PANTS FOR A MINIMALIST LOOK.

WHEN YOU'RE WEARING SOMETHING VERY GLAMOROUS, KEEP YOUR HANDBAG AND SHOES LOOKING VERY SIMPLE AND COOL.

PINK AND KHAKI OUTFITS RESEMBLE SAKURA MOCHI. I LOVE THEM.

I ALSO LOVE KANSAI-STYLE SAKURA MEOWCHI.

- Pink top
- Slim ankle-length khaki pants
- Strappy heeled black sandals
- Black bag

Navy and Khaki

NAVY AND KHAKI—A COMBINATION THAT MAKES YOU LOOK LIKE A REAL INTELLECTUAL!! I RECOMMEND THIS FOR A WORK OUTFIT.

A BLOUSE IN A SMOOTH, THIN RAYON MATERIAL AND A COOL COLOR TO MATCH THE NAVY GIVES OFF A REALLY LADYLIKE AURA.

- Airy Khaki Rayon Blouse
- Tapered Cotton Navy High-Water Pants
- Black Pumps
- Black Lycra tote

04 Keep logos the size of a stamp, no larger.

THIS IS A MICKEY MOUSE T-SHIRT THAT CAN BE BOUGHT AT A FAST FASHION SHOP. IF THE CHARACTER IS SMALL, YOU CAN INCORPORATE IT INTO YOUR EVERYDAY WARDROBE.

WHEN YOU'RE WEARING AN ITEM WITH A CARTOON CHARACTER ON IT, YOU CAN'T GO WRONG BY MAKING THE REST OF THE OUTFIT BLACK AND WHITE.

BAKER PANTS (OR FATIGUE PANTS) ARE BEST FOR THIS OUTFIT. THE THINNER THE PANT, THE MORE DIFFICULT IT IS TO CHOOSE A TOP!!

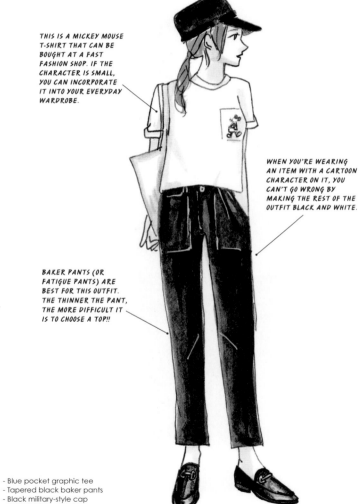

- Blue pocket graphic tee
- Tapered black baker pants
- Black military-style cap
- Black loafers
- Large white tote

As the years pile up, you start to think you can't wear clothes with cartoon characters, right? But if you wear them the right way, it can become a highlight of your outfit and you'll be seen as fashionable.

The more the character becomes the focus of the garment, the more your carefully polished adult image fades away. An embroidered embellishment is good enough, so let's go with the smallest size we can find.

The smaller the character, the longer you'll be able to wear the article of clothing.

It'll also be easier to put together more outfits using that garment, so in the end you win!

When you've decided to wear an item with a cartoon character on it, you'll want to match it up with more adult, sophisticated items of clothing. The best things to wear are collared polo shirts, pencil or denim skirts and sandals with heels.

WHEN YOU REALLY LOVE A CERTAIN DESIGN, YOU GET EXCITED WHEN YOU GET A CHANCE TO WEAR IT, DON'T YOU?
I'M PARTIAL TO THE SMILEY FACE...

A BLACK HOODIE AND A KHAKI SKIRT MAKE FOR A COMBINATION THAT GIVES YOU A CALMING AURA.

- Black cartoon-character polo shirt
- Denim button-up skirt
- Black heeled sandals
- Hooded sweatshirt

05 Buy a scarf.

AN OFF-THE-RACK BLOUSE AND A PAIR OF WIDE-LEGGED PANTS MAKE FOR A SHARP WORK OUTFIT.

CHUNKY HEELED BACKSTRAP SANDALS ARE EASY TO WALK IN, AND THEY ALWAYS LOOK CUTE. THEY'RE THE BEST!!

- Compact black cotton
  V-neck T-shirt
- Draped wide-leg blue pants
- Black chunky sandals
- White patent tote

With just a single scarf, my bag transforms!

Scarves are a very convenient item to have. An item you've had for ages can be transformed into something trendy in an instant!

Let's put away the idea of wearing a scarf around your neck and think of putting it somewhere else as the norm.

STEP 1

THIS BAG MATCHES EVERYTHING, BUT IT'S ON THE BORING SIDE.

WITH A BAG LIKE THIS, YOU CAN WRAP IT IN A SCARF LIKE THIS AND IT'S SUDDENLY SHOWY.

YOUR NORMAL BAG TRANSFORMS!

IT'S MUCH CHEAPER THAN BUYING A BUNCH OF BAGS, MEOW.

When choosing a scarf, the more colors, the better.

It's better to use irregular patterns than regular ones. Irregular patterns never look monotonous when they're tied on.

If you look for a scarf that uses even one of the colors from the rest of the outfit, you link up the colors and the outfit looks fashionable and well coordinated.

Learning how to tie a scarf is really important. If you tie it too loose, it could come undone over time.
Be careful.

If you're not interested in tying it to a bag, I also recommend using it as a belt!

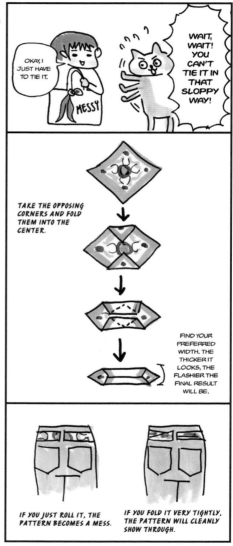

Try using it as a belt.

Lastly, let's give ourselves a chance to wear a scarf around our necks. Our next way of folding makes the surface area very small and gives the impression of a patterned top.

If you can only see a little bit of the scarf just at your neck, then you've got an attractive look!

A SCARF WITH BROWN ACCENTS WILL GIVE A CALM IMPRESSION, NO MATTER WHAT THE PATTERN IS.

BROWN ACCESSORIES ARE CRAZY FASHIONABLE!

A HARD-SIDED PURSE GIVES YOU A DIGNIFIED AIR AT WORK.

- Extra-fine black merino cowl-neck sweater
- Tan belt
- Patterned scarf
- Tan pumps

06

Buy men's clothing and you'll find something cool.

YOU'LL LOOK REFINED BY LAYERING BASIC ITEMS LIKE THIS BEIGE COAT, HOODIE AND STRIPED SHIRT.

RED PUMPS INSTANTLY MAKE AN OUTFIT MORE LADYLIKE. ♥

MHL.

- Tan knee-length overcoat
- Blue-striped white crew neck
  sweater (men's)
- Full-zip gray hooded sweatshirt (men's)
- High-rise cigarette jeans
- Red pumps
- Tote bag

If you master the ability to shop for men's clothing, you'll be able to find amazing items you would never have noticed before.

The trick is just to remember that a men's size medium is usually a women's size large.

However, men's sleeves tend to be too long on women, so let's go with half-sleeve shirts instead.

If you compare the women's section and the men's section at fast fashion stores, you'll see that men's sections tend to have many more basic items. In addition, men's sections tend to have color variations that women's sections don't. More colors are much more fun!

The merits of including men's clothing in your wardrobe are these:

THE LOOSENESS OF MEN'S SWEATSHIRTS GIVES YOU A VERY CUTE AIR.

IF YOU ROLL UP THE SLEEVES, THEY'RE INCREDIBLY WEARABLE.

GREY AND KHAKI TULLE SKIRTS ARE VERY APPEALING, AND THEY'RE PERFECT EVEN FOR ADULT WOMEN!

- Black pullover hooded sweatshirt (men's)
- High-waisted chiffon pleated skirt
- Tennis shoes

07 You only need three pairs of shoes.

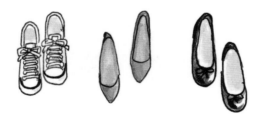

I have a bad habit of buying many different pairs of shoes without thinking about it. The important thing with shoes is making sure you understand your options. If you choose from just a few types of shoes, you can change the feel of your outfit and look much more fashionable without expending extra effort.

For most occasions, you only need to own these three pairs of shoes:

- black ballet shoes
- beige pumps
- white sneakers

The reason the pumps should be beige is that it's close to skin tone for some people. It makes your legs look long and slender. (Substitute a more appropriate color if your skin tone is different.)

If your shoes are all the same style but have different colors and designs, they can't be used in a variety of situations.

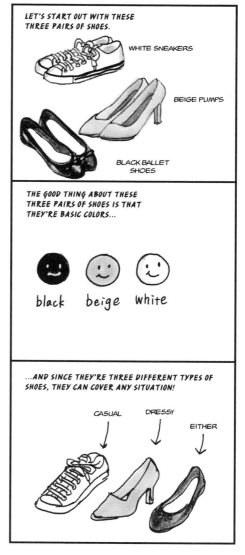

LET'S START OUT WITH THESE THREE PAIRS OF SHOES.

WHITE SNEAKERS

BEIGE PUMPS

BLACK BALLET SHOES

THE GOOD THING ABOUT THESE THREE PAIRS OF SHOES IS THAT THEY'RE BASIC COLORS...

black   beige   white

...AND SINCE THEY'RE THREE DIFFERENT TYPES OF SHOES, THEY CAN COVER ANY SITUATION!

CASUAL   DRESSY   EITHER

Of course, on top of these three styles, you'll want to have sandals for summer and boots for winter. After that, you can buy any kind of shoes you like without really thinking about it! Shoes that are bright colors like blue and pink work as a focal piece, but they're hard to match with a lot of different outfits, so don't buy them until you've got your three foundational pairs.

By changing your shoes, you can broaden your own possible outfits. The same lace skirt can feel completely different with different shoes.

MATCHING A LACE SKIRT WITH SNEAKERS, A CANVAS BAG AND A T-SHIRT MAKES THE WHOLE OUTFIT LOOK CASUAL DESPITE THE FACT THAT THE SKIRT IS FANCY.

- Black pocket T-shirt
- Green lace skirt
- White canvas sneakers
- Bordered tote

AN OUTFIT BUILT AROUND BALLET FLATS AND A BASKET-WOVEN BAG WITH BLACK ACCENTS FITS TOGETHER WELL.

- White T-shirt
- Denim jacket
- Green lace skirt
- Black ballet flats
- Woven tote

OTHER THAN THE SKIRT, EVERYTHING IN THIS OUTFIT IS VERY SIMPLE.

- White bell-sleeve top
- Green lace skirt
- Tan pumps
- Gray and tan tote

Here are some of the looks you can create with a striped shirt and jeans just by mixing up the shoes:

A STRIPED SWEATER IS MORE FANCY THAN A SIMILAR OFF-THE-RACK SHIRT!! PUTTING THAT TOGETHER WITH THE PUMPS BRINGS THE OUTFIT TO A NEW LEVEL BY MIXING CASUAL AND FANCY.

- Gray-striped crew neck long-sleeved white sweater
- High-rise straight-leg rolled-ankle jeans
- Tan pumps

WHEN YOU PAIR DENIM WITH SNEAKERS, A SHIRT TIED AROUND YOUR WAIST CAN REALLY EMPHASIZE THE LOOK. YOU CAN DO THIS PURPOSEFULLY TO CREATE A SENSE OF LIVELY BALANCE.

PAIR BALLET FLATS WITH A SMALL BAG AND CARDIGAN. BY SPREADING OUT THE BLACK ITEMS, YOU CAN GIVE THE OUTFIT A UNIFIED VIBE, EVEN IF THE BLACK ITEMS COVER A COMPARATIVELY SMALL AREA.

- Gray-striped crew neck long-sleeved white sweater
- High-rise straight-leg rolled-ankle jeans
- Checked flannel button-up
- Backpack
- Canvas sneakers

- Gray-striped crew neck long-sleeved white sweater
- High-rise straight-leg rolled-ankle jeans
- Black extrafine merino crewneck cardigan
- Black ballet flats

Here are some looks you can achieve by combining the three different shoe styles with a flannel dress. Just by changing the shoes you wear, you can get many more outfits out of the same clothes!

RIBBED LEGGINGS
AND SNEAKERS LOOK
MUCH MORE STYLISH
THAN TIGHTS.

- Plaid flannel one-piece dress
- Cotton twill cap
- Stretch down vest
- Ribbed leggings
- Canvas sneakers
- Tote bag

THE BLACK
BALLET FLATS
AND LIGHT GRAY
SOCKS MAKE THIS
A POWERFUL LOOK
FOR FALL.

BROWN TIGHTS PAIR
NATURALLY WITH
THE BEIGE PUMPS!

- Plaid flannel one-piece dress
- Neo leather biker jacket
- Pumps

- Plaid flannel one-piece dress
- Brown cardigan
- Black ballet flats
- Tan backpack

08 You don't have to try clothes on.

JUST WEARING A T-SHIRT
WITH FRILLY SLEEVES MAKES
YOU FEEL LIKE YOUR WHOLE
OUTFIT LOOKS SHARP.

TRY TYING A RIBBON
BELT ON THE SIDE AND
LETTING ONE OF THE
LOOSE ENDS DANGLE!!
IT MAKES THE BELLY
AREA LOOK MUCH
THINNER.

- Brown frilly-sleeve T-shirt
- Wide cotton ribbon-belted pants
- Black sandals
- White fringed bag

Sometimes it's a pain to try on clothes.

At those times, feel free to just buy your usual sizes.

People often say that each article of clothing is sized slightly differently from other, similar items. They say that you should try them on just in case, but to be honest, similar items are mostly the same.

People sometimes say it's cute to wear a larger size because it's baggy, but in order to wear a larger size and not look like you've gained weight, you have to pay a lot of attention to the other parts of the outfit. In the end, it's often easier to just buy your usual size.

09 How to master wearing loose clothing without trying it on.

So, what do you do when you want to wear your clothes nice and loose?

At times like that, you want to get clothing in your usual size that is designed to be loose.

Clothing brands often make clothes that are meant to hang loose and look cute, but that follow the normal sizes.

The items at a shop that are labeled "oversized" are items that are meant to fit loosely from the start.

When you put one of these on, you may become super stylish!

STRIPED TOPS LIKE THIS ONE GIVE YOU A BOXY SILHOUETTE THAT'S FULLY ON TREND RIGHT NOW!! IT PAIRS WELL WITH ANYTHING, INCLUDING WIDE PANTS AND SKIRTS.

- Striped wide T-shirt

DROP SHOULDER KNITS REALLY TAKE THE EMPHASIS OFF YOUR SHOULDERS AND ARE EASY TO WEAR.

- Ribbed red drop shoulder sweater

A KNIT SWEATER WITH TULLE SLEEVES IS THE KIND OF MULTIMATERIAL GARMENT THAT GOES WELL WITH SIMPLE ITEMS IN A SUBTRACTIVE STYLE.

LET'S MATCH UP WIDE PANTS MADE FROM A TOUGH MATERIAL WITH A BLOUSE MADE FROM A SOFT MATERIAL! ♥

- Tulle sleeve vertical-striped sweater

- Spotted yellow box collar shirt

10 Buy your white items cheaply.

WHEN YOU WEAR A KNITTED CASHMERE STOLE AROUND YOUR NECK AND A FLUFFY KNIT BAG, THE DIFFERENCES IN THEIR RESPECTIVE MATERIALS CAN CREATE A COMPLEX AND EYE-CATCHING LOOK.

A LOOSE IVORY KNIT SWEATER WITH AN ACCORDION-PLEATED SKIRT MAKES FOR A UNIQUELY WINTER-THEMED OUTFIT. LONG AND NARROW OUTFITS MAKE AN I-LINE SILHOUETTE THAT IS FLATTERING TO MOST FIGURES.

- Pleated black spotted skirt
- Side panel boots
- White knit tote bag

White is a special color. It conveys an impression of cleanliness, looks good with most skin tones and gives you a young appearance. White can make women look more beautiful and charming.

The only drawback of white is that it shows stains very easily. That's why it's best not to spend a lot of money on white items.

If you check out fast fashion shops, you'll be able to get most of your items for under 50 dollars.

There are two types of white. White with a bluish tinge gives a cool, refreshing impression, while off-white has a gentleness and a warmth.

Cool bluish white

An off-white with warmth to it

There are a number of wonderful things that come to mind when you think of white.

PEARLS

SNOW

WEDDING DRESSES

WHITE COATS

CHILLED TOFU

RICE

SOFT SERVE

HEH HEH HEH

RARE CHEESES

BABY'S BREATH

When you wear white, you associate those things with yourself!

When your white items get so dirty that putting them in the laundry just won't do it, replacing them may be a good solution.

When my clothes from fast fashion outlets get dirty, I donate them to a recycling center. They can be recycled no matter where they came from.

This is when you should toss your white clothing:

SHIRTS

WHEN THERE ARE YELLOWISH STAINS ON THE COLLAR THAT DON'T COME OUT IN THE WASH.

BAGS

WHEN THERE ARE YELLOWISH STAINS ON THE HANDLE.

MAISON KITSUNE
PARIS FRANCE

WHEN THE HEELS GET WORN DOWN. IT'S A SHAME WHEN THE LOGO STARTS TO RUB OFF.

WHITE SNEAKERS

YELLOWISH

T-SHIRTS

WHEN THE HEM AND THE SLEEVES GET THESE WOBBLY CURVES ON THEM, IT LOOKS VERY UNCOOL.

WHITE PANTS

WHEN THEY GET EVEN SMALL STAINS THAT CAN'T BE WASHED OUT.

11

If you want cutting edge designs, buy the things at the front of the store.

The trendiest items tend to be at the entrance of the store, closest to the front.

If you want to buy something at the cutting edge of fashion, shop near the entrance.

Items that are no longer in season are often greatly reduced in price. But wearing these clothes often requires buying other items. It's a pain, so just don't buy them.

Seasonal items can only be worn at specific times of the year, so try not to choose items that come with accompanying expenses. Instead, find something that is easy to coordinate with.

12 Remember to pair denim with your girliest articles of clothing.

RIBBED CAMISOLES THAT ARE SOLD AT FAST FASHION SHOPS HAVE CUTE DESIGNS AND DON'T LOOK TOO MUCH LIKE INTIMATE APPAREL EVEN WHEN THEY SHOW THROUGH.

LINEN SHIRTS ARE WELL SUITED TO ADULT WEAR!! THEY COME IN A VARIETY OF PRETTY SHADES.

A TOTE BAG FOLDED IN HALF AND CARRIED IN THE HAND LIKE A CLUTCH IS VERY FASHIONABLE!

- Pink linen shirt
- High-rise black cigarette jeans
- Black strappy heels
- Tote bag

Denim was once the main fabric in work clothes, so wearing it with other items can look very casual.

If you know this one trick to wearing denim, you'll look stylish every day with no effort! The trick is easy!

When you wear jeans, pair them with more fashionable items.

Wear...

Knits, not sweatshirts

Shoes that show your ankles instead of sneakers

Blouses and button-ups over T-shirts

Hats over ballcaps

Shoulder bags over backpacks

Even just changing one of these items to be more femme can transform your denim garment into something more than just work clothes.

13 A divine blouse does not wrinkle.

HALF SLEEVES CAN BE ROLLED UP, MAKING THEM NICE AND WIDE TO LET THE BREEZE IN SO YOU CAN STAY COOL.

CIRCULAR SKIRTS ARE MADE WITH A LOT OF FABRIC, SO THEY PUFF OUT WITH VOLUME AND ARE REALLY GORGEOUS!!

POLKA-DOTTED ITEMS IN BLACK AND WHITE GIVE YOU A COMBINATION OF FEMININITY AND MATURITY THAT IS HARD TO BEAT.

- Draped T-shirt blouse
- Black-and-white polka dot circular skirt
- Black tote

Ironing is such a pain, isn't it?

But if you have clothes that don't wrinkle, you don't have to iron anything! It's very easy. You should seek out wrinkle-free items.

I recommend work clothing that drapes around your figure. You can find affordable draped clothing that's glossy, looks expensive, won't get wrinkled and dries easily, even. There are nothing but positives with this choice!

WEARING A WELL-FITTED, GRAY ONE-BUTTON JACKET CAN GIVE EVEN A YOUNG PERSON A SOFT, APPROACHABLE IMAGE.

- Draped V-neck blouse
- Narrow checked skirt
- Stretch tailored gray jacket
- Black pumps
- White tote

You can wear many different kinds of shirts under a jacket. With shirts with no sleeves, you don't need to worry about the sleeves bunching, and shirts with no collar can go with any jacket no matter what kind.

DRAPED V-NECK BLOUSE

WHEN IT'S HOT, IT'S BEST TO WEAR THE SLEEVELESS SHIRT ALONG WITH A MAXI SKIRT. THE SMOOTH DRAPE FABRIC MEANS THAT EVEN IF YOU SHOW A LITTLE SKIN, IT DOESN'T LOOK IMPROPER.

DRAPED T-SHIRT BLOUSE

ROUNDED SLEEVES ON THE SHIRT SIDE CAN BE WORN UNCOVERED AND WILL LOOK VERY CUTE.

These items can be used just like T-shirts, but they provide a more glamorous finish. If you have children, you can wear these outfits to school events and similar functions where you feel like you haven't gotten a chance to show off your best. Using these suggestions will help.

- Paper fedora hat
- Draped V-neck blouse
- Black strappy sandals
- Shoulder bag

- Red draped T-shirt blouse
- High-rise cigarette jeans
- Black slip-ons
- Shoulder bag

14

Feel free to ignore the season's trendy color.

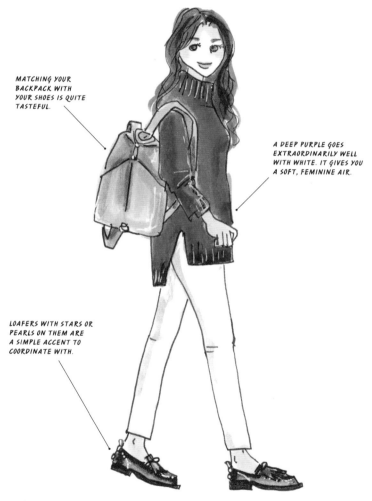

MATCHING YOUR BACKPACK WITH YOUR SHOES IS QUITE TASTEFUL.

A DEEP PURPLE GOES EXTRAORDINARILY WELL WITH WHITE. IT GIVES YOU A SOFT, FEMININE AIR.

LOAFERS WITH STARS OR PEARLS ON THEM ARE A SIMPLE ACCENT TO COORDINATE WITH.

- White thermal leggings
- Loafers
- Gray backpack

Different colors are in style every year. You'll think, "I keep seeing these same colors in stores and magazines all over the place." All at once, you'll see a lot of the same colors in new products.

Which means that not wearing the season's color can actually be pretty stylish.

Not every color looks good on every person. Try to avoid wearing something that's not your color!

If you just wear the most trendy clothing designs in your color, you will look as fashionable as you need to look. It'll also be more likely to suit you.

Prioritize design over color and buy trendy designs in your favorite or neutral colors.

15 Design flourishes on sleeves or the neckline, never both.

IN THE SUMMER, WHEN YOU DON'T HAVE TO WEAR AS MANY LAYERS, TRY CARRYING A BAG WITH A VERY STRONG IMPACT LIKE THIS ONE.

WITH WIDE PANTS, BE SURE TO WEAR TOPS THAT ARE ON THE SHORT SIDE. JUST BY DOING THAT, YOU'LL END UP WITH A VERY TRENDY SILHOUETTE.

- Purple knit sweater
- High-waisted green chinos
- Smiley face woven bag

Here's what you need to know about how to wear cute tops:

Only have a design flourish on your collar or your sleeves, never both.

Just remember that and you should be all right.

Look a little more stylish without much effort just by wearing full sleeves. Full sleeves also have many other merits:

YOUR UPPER ARMS DON'T SHOW TOO OBVIOUSLY.

YOU LOOK GORGEOUS, EVEN WITHOUT ACCESSORIES.

AS YOU GROW OLDER, YOUR SKIN THINS AT YOUR DE-COLLETAGE SO KEEP THINGS A LITTLE HIDDEN.

YOU'LL LOOK THINNER.

FULL SLEEVES ARE THE BEST!

IT'S TOO HOT FOR THIS!

FLARED SLEEVES CAN
GIVE YOUR OUTFIT A
FANCY, FLOWERY FEEL.

LONG-HEMMED, WIDE-LEGGED
OVERALLS CAN BE WORN EVEN
BY ADULT WOMEN WITHOUT
PEOPLE GETTING TOO RILED
UP ABOUT THEM.

- Pink crepe jersey flared-sleeve T-shirt
- Black ribbon belted overall jumpsuit
- Pink loafers

16

Fashionable people only buy three types of purses.

I think there are a lot of people out there who, without thinking about it, manage to accumulate a number of the exact same type of bags in their homes.

If you get all your bags together, you should have at least three types:

- a light-colored backpack
- a large shoulder bag
- a handbag with a long chain or strap

These three bags represent completely different styles, so you'll never have a reason to say, "I don't have the right purse for this outfit!"

First, a light-colored backpack.

A light color will look cool in the summer, and since a lot of outerwear in winter has desaturated colors, it won't look strange with those either. White is a good choice.

Next is a large shoulder bag or tote.

THE MOST IMPORTANT
THING IS THAT IT'S NOT
TOO HEAVY! ALSO, SINCE
THIS KIND OF BAG IS MADE
FROM THE SAME MATERIAL
AS A WETSUIT, IT CAN BE
WASHED INSIDE AND OUT,
WHICH ARE POINTS IN ITS
FAVOR. ❤

THIS KIND OF BAG
IS DURABLE. IT'S
A SIMPLE DESIGN
THAT CAN BE
CARRIED BY MEN
OR WOMEN.

TOTE BAGS CAN BE PURCHASED
AT CHEAP PRICES, AND THAT
MAKES ME HAPPY.

You can add seasonal accessories to your bag instead of buying new
bags every season. It makes it all much cheaper.

The final type of bag you need is one with a long chain or strap. Of the three bags, this one may see the least amount of use, but having one is very useful. It does its best work on the days you go the furthest out of your comfort zone.

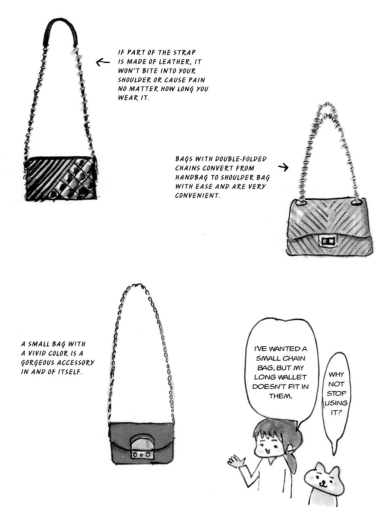

← IF PART OF THE STRAP IS MADE OF LEATHER, IT WON'T BITE INTO YOUR SHOULDER OR CAUSE PAIN NO MATTER HOW LONG YOU WEAR IT.

BAGS WITH DOUBLE-FOLDED CHAINS CONVERT FROM HANDBAG TO SHOULDER BAG WITH EASE AND ARE VERY CONVENIENT. →

A SMALL BAG WITH A VIVID COLOR IS A GORGEOUS ACCESSORY IN AND OF ITSELF.

I'VE WANTED A SMALL CHAIN BAG, BUT MY LONG WALLET DOESN'T FIT IN THEM.

WHY NOT STOP USING IT?

Here are a few times when having a strappy handbag is great:

Party

IT WON'T GET IN THE WAY, EVEN IF YOU HANG IT OFF THE BACK OF YOUR CHAIR.

A Girl's Night

CARRYING ONLY A FEW ITEMS IS FASHIONABLE.

Traveling

IT'S NICE TO HAVE BOTH HANDS FREE.

Not only can these three bags be paired with any outfit—with them, you'll be able to change the feel of an outfit just by switching bags! Give it a try.

A hard-sided square tote bag is good for work. I recommend using a canvas bag if you're carrying things for your children.

When you think you need a new outfit because you don't have anything nice to wear out, just try wearing a strapped handbag with your regular clothes. You'll hardly recognize yourself.

17

You can never go wrong with a skirt that's long and narrow.

IN EARLY FALL, WEAR A HALF-SLEEVE SWEATER AND CARRY A CARDIGAN SO YOU CAN REGULATE YOUR BODY HEAT EVEN WHEN THE TEMPERATURE FLUCTUATES A LOT.

CORDUROY IS A RIDGED FABRIC WITH A WINTERY OR AUTUMNAL ATMOSPHERE.

MATCHING A FRONT-BUTTON SKIRT WITH SIMPLE ARTICLES OF CLOTHING BRINGS AN OUTFIT TOGETHER IN A WAY THAT MAKES IT BEAUTIFUL.

- Extra-fine black merino V-neck cardigan
- Corduroy front-buttoned skirt
- Brown pumps
- Feather-trimmed bag

Have you ever thought, "This skirt doesn't look good on me anymore"?

The trick to choosing a good skirt is surprisingly simple.

Just look for a long-hemmed skirt that doesn't flare out.

Of course, it's great to be able to wear whatever kinds of clothes you love. Unfortunately, there are clothes in this world that just will not suit you. Putting together an outfit with those clothes in such a way that they do suit you is probably one of fashion's greatest pleasures, but when it's too much of a pain to do that, make sure to have some long skirts on hand just in case.

If you want to look sexy, your best choice is to wear a long skirt with a deep slit along the side. It looks sophisticated and beautiful.

If you're going for a casual look, a narrow skirt will still look dignified.

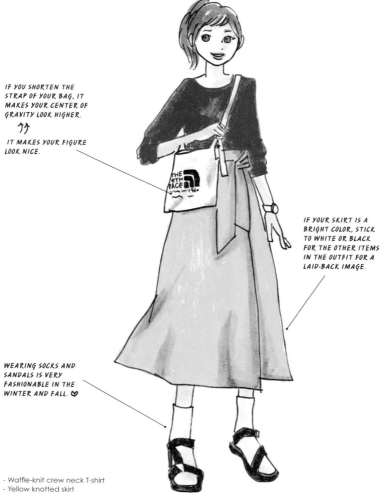

IF YOU SHORTEN THE STRAP OF YOUR BAG, IT MAKES YOUR CENTER OF GRAVITY LOOK HIGHER.

IT MAKES YOUR FIGURE LOOK NICE.

IF YOUR SKIRT IS A BRIGHT COLOR, STICK TO WHITE OR BLACK FOR THE OTHER ITEMS IN THE OUTFIT FOR A LAID-BACK IMAGE.

WEARING SOCKS AND SANDALS IS VERY FASHIONABLE IN THE WINTER AND FALL. ❤

- Waffle-knit crew neck T-shirt
- Yellow knotted skirt
- Black sandals
- Shoulder tote

18 Navy blue striped shirts are better than plain white shirts.

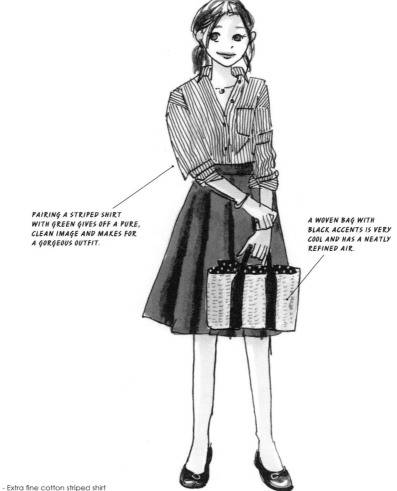

PAIRING A STRIPED SHIRT WITH GREEN GIVES OFF A PURE, CLEAN IMAGE AND MAKES FOR A GORGEOUS OUTFIT.

A WOVEN BAG WITH BLACK ACCENTS IS VERY COOL AND HAS A NEATLY REFINED AIR.

- Extra fine cotton striped shirt
- High-waisted sweat-wicking green stretch skirt
- Black ballet flats
- Wicker bag with black ribbon

They say that no woman looks bad in a white shirt, but is that really true?

If it fits too tightly...

I LOOK SERIOUS...

It can also look too puffy.

I LOOK LIKE A CHEF.

It's important to account for the "school uniform" effect when wearing a white shirt.

On the other hand, a navy striped shirt works perfectly.

Navy and white together create a fresh aesthetic. They look sophisticated, without a hint of a school uniform vibe. The thin stripes deliver a feminine energy, and the flowing silhouette makes things look casual. Being both feminine and casual means you can coordinate the shirt with many different outfits. Buy items in cotton for a clean, minimalist look.

Please try adding a navy pinstripe button-up to your own wardrobe!
This shirt goes well with any style of outfit, including office and
casual ones.

CARRYING A SILVER
BAG WITH AN
OUTFIT THAT IS
MOSTLY BLACK ADDS
SOMETHING BRIGHT.

WEARING A KNIT
DRESS OVER THE
SHIRT IS REALLY
CUTE. ♥

- Extra-fine cotton
  striped shirt
- Knit black dress
- Ribbed leggings
- Black ballet flats
- Holographic silver bag

WEARING A
STRIPED SHIRT
WITH CHINOS
CREATES A
RELAXED AIR
AND A VERY
COOL OUTFIT.

WHEN WEARING
CHINO PANTS
THAT RESEMBLE
MENSWEAR, CHOOSE
LARGE EARRINGS
INSTEAD OF SMALL
ONES.

A FRINGED BAG AND
LEATHER SHOES CAN
LOOK MUCH MORE
FEMININE WHEN
WORN IN WHITE.

- Extra-fine cotton striped shirt
- Cotton tapered chino pants
- White leather shoes
- Fringed white leather handbag

19 Make sure to wear small accessories.

WHEN YOU MATCH THE VISUAL AESTHETICS OF YOUR NECKLACE AND EARRINGS, THE JEWELRY WILL STAND OUT, MAKING YOU LOOK MUCH MORE FASHIONABLE. ↑↑

WEAR A LONG NECKLACE WITH A BOATNECK SHIRT THAT IS OPEN ON THE SIDES. IT CREATES A VERTICAL LINE THAT MAKES YOU LOOK SHAPELY.

IN THE WINTER, I RECOMMEND WEARING HOOP EARRINGS! POST EARRINGS MAY RUB AGAINST YOUR HOOD OR SCARF AND TEAR OFF, BUT WITH HOOPS THAT'S NOT A WORRY AT ALL!!

As the years pile up, the shine of your skin and hair fades. That shine is what makes people look younger. This problem can be solved with the power of accessories.

The sparkle of accessories supplements your shine where it's lacking.

You should try wearing one of the three types of earrings or clip-ons on the next page every day. If you don't habitually wear earrings but would like to start, you may want to begin with wearing them every night. Eventually, you'll get used to them!

WHAT ADULT WOMEN NEED IN ORDER TO REALLY SPARKLE IS NOT EXPENSIVE SKIN TONERS BUT ACCESSORIES!

THERE ARE MANY PEOPLE WHO DON'T KNOW THAT NO MATTER HOW SMALL YOUR EARRINGS ARE, THEY REFLECT THE LIGHT THAT SHINES ON THEM AND GIVE YOU A GLOW.

IN RESTAURANTS AND CAFES WITH A DARK ATMOSPHERE, OLDER WOMEN ARE AT A DISADVANTAGE.

MIWAKO, YOU LOOK SCARY.

YOU TOO, NODOKA.

Pearl

PEARLS WITH A BOATNECK MAKE A VERY POWERFUL COMBINATION!

Dangling earrings

WEARING DANGLING EARRINGS WITH A DRESS SHIRT AND JEANS ADDS A FEMININE TOUCH TO AN OTHERWISE SIMPLE OUTFIT.

THEY'RE VERY DELICATE, SO THEY DON'T STAND OUT, EVEN IN AN OFFICE SETTING.

THEY MUST HAVE A VERY NARROW DESIGN.

Hoops

WEARING THEM WITH A BLACK-AND-WHITE OUTFIT GIVES A SOFT ACCENT TO YOUR IMAGE.

LARGE HOOPS ARE MORE CASUAL AND SMALL HOOPS ARE A BIT MORE FEMININE.

Silver earrings give you a cool image. Gold has a warmth to it, which makes it a little more showy and gorgeous.

These three types of earrings are small and don't attract too much attention, so they can be worn with any sort of outfit. If you don't want to spend a lot of time deciding which to wear, pick any pair and you'll be fine.

Wearing accessories is like weight training. If you're making sure to do it every day, you won't have any issues, even on days when you want to look especially nice. These are examples of the things you'll learn by wearing accessories every day:

If you wear earrings every day, you'll get to the point where you can wear larger earrings without fear.

20 If you buy a necklace, make sure it's one you wouldn't mind wearing every day.

Necklaces give you the same kind of shine that earrings do, and make your skin look shinier.

There are two types of necklace that are good to have around:

I RECOMMEND TWO NECKLACES, ONE WITH A SHORT CHAIN AND ONE WITH A LONG ONE. MAKE SURE THAT THE PENDANT IS NO LARGER THAN THE NAIL ON YOUR THUMB.

JUST MAKE SURE IT'S NO LARGER THAN THIS.

WHAT DO YOU WANT—GOLD, SILVER, COPPER?

JUST TAKE AS MANY AS YOU WANT.

WHAT'RE YOU SAYING? DON'T BE SO CHEAP!

SO GENEROUS! BUT NO, NO!

SQUISH

MEOW...

WHAT I WANT IS TO LOOK FASHIONABLE, EASILY AND CHEAPLY!

A small necklace will give you a sparkle and an effortless shine. Try it out to make your skin look beautiful.

A small necklace can match with just about anything, so they don't take any time on mornings when you're having trouble choosing clothes. That's one of their good points. Also, they really raise your fashion level.

Having two necklaces that you're very fond of is plenty.

Of course, for those of you who don't stress out when choosing a necklace to wear at a party or an event, you can easily wear a flashy or large necklace, or even a necklace with an artistic flourish.

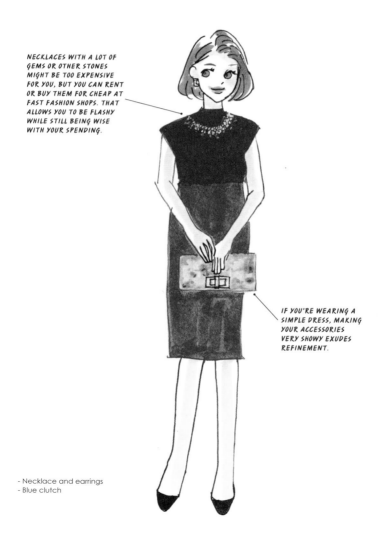

NECKLACES WITH A LOT OF GEMS OR OTHER STONES MIGHT BE TOO EXPENSIVE FOR YOU, BUT YOU CAN RENT OR BUY THEM FOR CHEAP AT FAST FASHION SHOPS. THAT ALLOWS YOU TO BE FLASHY WHILE STILL BEING WISE WITH YOUR SPENDING.

IF YOU'RE WEARING A SIMPLE DRESS, MAKING YOUR ACCESSORIES VERY SHOWY EXUDES REFINEMENT.

- Necklace and earrings
- Blue clutch

Even if you don't want to, make sure to have things hemmed at the shop.

You may tell yourself, "I'll come back to have it hemmed another day," but you never will. So, when you buy pants, be sure to have them hemmed at the store when they offer it. Think of it as part of the purchase itself.

21

When choosing a flower pattern to wear, make sure it's large, not small.

WHY NOT TRY WEARING A WHITE T-SHIRT WITH A WIDE NECKLINE UNDER AN OPEN BUTTON-FRONT DRESS? JUXTAPOSING YOUR SKIN AND FLOWERS GIVES YOU A HEALTHY LOOK.

WEARING JEANS AND SNEAKERS WOULD NORMALLY SEEM PRETTY CASUAL, BUT THE SLIGHTLY SEE-THROUGH FLOWER DRESS GIVES YOU A FEMININE AIR WITH NO EFFORT.

- Two-way ribbed tee
- High-rise cigarette jeans
- White slip-on sneakers
- Tote

Flower patterns make you look bright and gorgeous. It's got nothing to do with current trends.

However, since small flower patterns can come off as cloying and cutesy, try medium or large flower patterns so you can look pretty without being too precious.

Also, be sure to go with a hem that's a little longer. No matter the color or pattern, it should be fine.

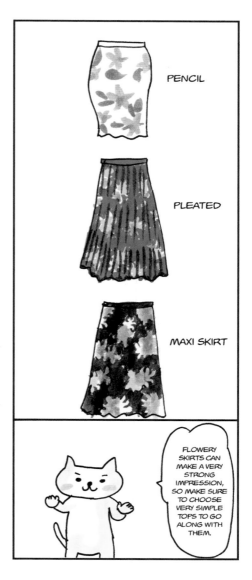

PENCIL

PLEATED

MAXI SKIRT

FLOWERY SKIRTS CAN MAKE A VERY STRONG IMPRESSION, SO MAKE SURE TO CHOOSE VERY SIMPLE TOPS TO GO ALONG WITH THEM.

In the summer, wearing flower-print clothing and carrying a woven bag is incredibly stylish.

SINCE FLOWER-PATTERN SKIRTS HAVE A HUGE IMPACT, MAKE SURE TO ONLY WEAR TOPS IN BASIC, SIMPLE COLORS.

MAKE SURE TO CHOOSE A SKIRT WITH A LONG HEM AND A LARGE PATTERN! THE COLOR AND PATTERN TYPE IS UP TO YOU.

ok

- Linen-blend white blouse
- Large flower-pattern skirt
- Black sandals
- Tan square woven handbag

- Black-and-white flowered skirt
- White slip-on sneakers
- Black basket-woven purse

In winter, when colors tend to get darker, flower patterns can be attention getting.

A MIDI SKIRT WORN WITH EITHER A SHORT JACKET

OR A LONG JACKET

WILL MAKE YOUR FIGURE LOOK NICE.

WOOL SKIRTS AND JACKETS ARE MADE OF THICK FABRIC, SO YOUR OUTFIT WILL LOOK WARM AND COZY. IT'S WONDERFUL.

- Neo leather black jacket
- Black cashmere crew neck sweater
- Green flowered skirt
- Black boots

- Gray long wool jacket
- Yellow flowered skirt
- Pumps

Next, let's try working a floral-pattern one-piece dress into our wardrobe.

THE TRICK TO WEARING THESE DRESSES IS TO REDUCE THE AMOUNT OF THE DRESS YOU CAN SEE!!

DIRECT

IF ALL YOU EVER WEAR ARE FLOWERED DRESSES, YOU'LL LOOK THE SAME, NO MATTER HOW YOU ACCESSORIZE THEM.

Wear a cardigan or a sweatshirt over the top instead.

WEARING A SWEATSHIRT THAT LOOKS A LITTLE LIKE A MEN'S GARMENT GIVES YOU A COOL EDGE.

A LOOSELY KNIT CARDIGAN AND SHEEPSKIN BOOTS GIVE YOU A SOFT AND GENTLE APPEARANCE.

- Black sweatshirt
- Tan canvas sneakers
- Black woven tote

- Tan loose-knit cardigan
- Fuzzy boots

22 Fitted pants should be hemmed on the shorter side.

A LIGHT-PURPLE COAT WILL MATCH WHATEVER YOU WANT TO WEAR IT WITH, MUCH LIKE A WHITE COAT. GO WILD!

ANKLE-LENGTH PANTS WITH SOCKS AND BALLET FLATS GIVE ANY OUTFIT A FASHION BOOST.

- Light-purple coat
- White mock turtleneck sweater
- Belt
- High-rise cigarette jeans
- Plaid black-and-white ballet flats

Fitted pants that are hemmed on the short side add an air of refinement.

Hem your fitted pants to the point where your ankle is fully visible when you wear them.

Tip #2 How to dry shirts without having to iron them.

Isn't it a huge pain to iron all your clothes? Let me tell you a trick I came up with that will allow you to go without ironing some of your clothing.

23 The most fashionable colors for socks are white and gray.

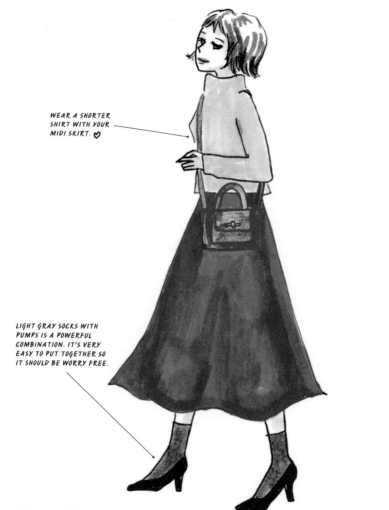

WEAR A SHORTER SHIRT WITH YOUR MIDI SKIRT. ♡

LIGHT GRAY SOCKS WITH PUMPS IS A POWERFUL COMBINATION. IT'S VERY EASY TO PUT TOGETHER SO IT SHOULD BE WORRY FREE.

- Yellow mock turtleneck sweater
- Blue midi skirt
- Black pumps

In the winter, the problem with wearing ankle-cut pants is exposing your ankles. When it's cold, there's no good reason to show off your bare skin, so why not put on some socks? If you remember these techniques for wearing socks, you'll feel warm and fashionable. You can even use socks as the focal piece of a whole outfit. That should broaden your style horizons!

Of course, you can mess up
with socks, too...

If you don't want to make mistakes like this, I would put off buying socks with patterns on them altogether. The most important kinds of socks to buy are foolproof colors like gray and white.

They match with any clothes and will look stylish no matter what.

With these three colors, you can just choose whichever socks you like and they will definitely match your outfit. You want to buy them because they're boring colors. The convenience these boring colors bring means you can wear them often.

In spring and fall, during the time when the seasons are changing over, wearing socks with sandals can be very cute.

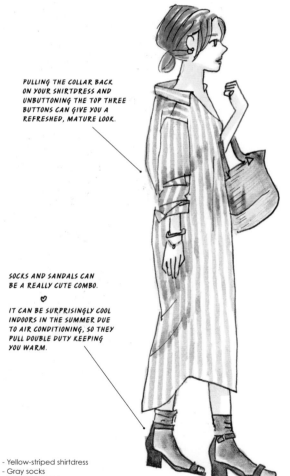

PULLING THE COLLAR BACK ON YOUR SHIRTDRESS AND UNBUTTONING THE TOP THREE BUTTONS CAN GIVE YOU A REFRESHED, MATURE LOOK.

SOCKS AND SANDALS CAN BE A REALLY CUTE COMBO.

♡

IT CAN BE SURPRISINGLY COOL INDOORS IN THE SUMMER DUE TO AIR CONDITIONING, SO THEY PULL DOUBLE DUTY KEEPING YOU WARM.

- Yellow-striped shirtdress
- Gray socks
- Strappy sandals
- Two-tone wicker bag

24 When wearing loose pants, always wear short tops.

A T-SHIRT BLOUSE MADE OF DRAPE MATERIAL WILL FLOW AND SWAY AND HAS A REAL SHINE. IT'S A PRODUCT THAT ALWAYS LOOKS TOP QUALITY. WIDE PANTS ALSO INCREASE THE BEAUTY OF YOUR OUTFIT.

FLAT SANDALS WITH STRAPS MADE OF THIN MATERIAL MAKE YOUR FEET LOOK A LITTLE LONGER.

- Red drape T-shirt blouse
- High-waisted wide-legged pants
- Flat-black strappy sandals
- Dark wicker handbag

The best tops to pair with wide pants are short ones. Wide pants add a lot of volume on your lower half and wearing shorter tops balances that out. Of course, you can always tuck your shirts in…

But if you only tuck in the front, or if your shirt is made of a billowy, blousing fabric, you may need to tuck it in repeatedly as you go about your day. If you'd rather not have to do that, make sure you have some cropped-hem tops around—that's the easiest way to look fashionable.

Short tops are a convenient, easy way to balance out your outfit. Make sure to pick a shirt that covers about half of your belly.

25 Buy skirts with dark blue in their patterns.

WAFFLE-KNIT TOPS ARE AS AFFORDABLE AS SWEATSHIRTS BUT LOOK AS SHARP AS OTHER KNITS, SO THEY ARE A GREAT OPTION.

WHEN YOU WEAR A LONG SKIRT, I RECOMMEND SLIP-ON SHOES. WITH NO LACES, THEY LOOK A LOT MORE REFINED THAN SNEAKERS.

- Waffle-knit crew neck top
- Wrap striped skirt
- Black slip-on canvas sneakers
- Handled tote

I recommend buying any patterns with navy blue in them that you find.

Honestly, there's nothing that doesn't go well with a pattern that has navy blue in it.

Items with a pattern that includes navy blue look very elegant matched with gray and white. They match red, green and yellow items as well.

RED ADDS FEMININITY AND BRIGHTNESS TO AN OUTFIT.

WHITE COORDINATES WELL WITH MANY THINGS AND CAN MAKE YOU LOOK ELEGANT.

GREEN GIVES AN OUTFIT A DOWN-TO-EARTH, INTELLECTUAL VIBE.

YELLOW ADDS ENERGY AND LIVELINESS.

- Shiny V-neck cropped sweater
- Navy plaid skirt
- Black boots
- Black fur-accented handbag

26 When wearing voluminous clothing, tie up your hair.

IF YOUR TOPS AND BOTTOMS ARE BOTH VERY VOLUMINOUS, BE SURE TO CHOOSE THE SMALLEST PURSE YOU CAN.

A COLLARLESS OUTER GARMENT, LIKE A LONG CARDIGAN OR A COLLARLESS COAT, GIVES YOUR FIGURE A SLIM PROFILE.

WIDE PANTS THAT HANG TO THE TOPS OF YOUR FEET MAKES YOUR LEGS LOOK LONGER.

- Yellow wide pants
- Purple flats
- Purple shoulder bag

- White wool overcoat
- Crew neck blue-striped
  T-shirt (men's)
- Wide velour pants
- Pink ballet flats
- Cashmere stole

An outfit of all billowy, voluminous clothing can make you look like you've gained weight because no part of you will look slim.

Try showing your neck or ankles.

When wearing voluminous clothes it's important to consider the other aspects of your outfit. Specifically, your hair and shoes. Tie your hair up, and make sure that your shoes show off the tops and sides of your feet. Just try to make it look effortless and it'll be fine.

An outfit that is loose everywhere except for the neck and feet will make you look dainty, and your body will look slimmer!

Again, there are two tips to wearing a voluminous outfit:

• Wear a pair of shoes that show off the tops of your feet and you'll look sharp!

• Make sure you tie your hair into an updo.

27 Button-front shirt dresses look powerful.

REMOVING THE CLOTH BELT THAT COMES WITH YOUR SHIRT DRESS MAKES YOUR WHOLE OUTFIT LOOK MUCH MORE CASUAL.

A CIRCULAR BAG WILL ADD BOTH FEMININITY AND CLASS TO YOUR OUTFIT. IT'S A CONVENIENT ITEM FOR ANY LOOK!

LEGGINGS MADE OF RIBBED FABRIC IN A LIGHT BEIGE OR GRAY FEEL SUMMERY AND REFRESHING.

- Blue cotton shirt dress
- Black ribbed lace tank top
- Circular woven handbag
- Light-beige ribbed leggings

There's one specific dress that I recommend you own because of the impact it can bring to your outfits! That would be a button-front shirt dress. Please get one of these for yourself!

When you're trying to pick out a dress, check to see if these things are true:

• It can be fully unbuttoned
• It has a ribbon or belt for the waist
• It has a hem that ends below the knees

If you see a dress that has all of these things, buy it without delay. If it fulfills all these criteria, it doesn't even matter what pattern it has!

This one dress can be worn in so many different ways. If you tire of wearing it on its own, you can always try one of these!

- Take out the belt and wear it loosely draped as an outer item.

- Unbutton all the buttons and wear it as an open overcoat.

• Tie the belt and wear it with a pair of fitted pants.

• Of course, it's best to wear it as a single dress! If you want to wear it with a different belt, you'll want to wear that belt in a higher position, at your waist, even though belt loops are usually low.

28

Even if your clothes from ten years ago still fit, your body shape has changed.

Nodoka Magazine

BASIC ITEM

How many items do you own that you can wear all your life? The most important thing is that you like what you're buying. But if you look at the bottom line, it's just not sensible to spend a lot of money to buy only one item. Instead, buying things at a cheap price every so often is ultimately going to make you look more fashionable.

If people don't exercise, their muscles deteriorate as the years go on.

Buying things cheaply about once every three years is probably your best bet.

29

Limit your accent colors to the colors found in a twelve-piece set of colored pencils.

A SINGLE-COLOR OUTFIT WITH DARK BLUE CAN BE EFFORTLESSLY ENHANCED BY THE ADDITION OF A WHITE T-SHIRT FOR A CAREFREE FEEL ALONG WITH A CLEAN LOOK.

I RECOMMEND A YELLOW BAG WITH A BASIC TRENCH COAT AND JEANS. IT MAKES AN OUTFIT ENERGETIC AND LIVELY.

WEAR HIGH-TOPS WITH YOUR ANKLE-LENGTH PANTS!! YOU CAN GET THE BALANCED STYLISHNESS THAT YOU WANT VERY EASILY WITH THAT.

- Khaki trench coat
- Navy cashmere V-neck sweater
- Black ankle pants
- White canvas high-top sneakers

If you match basic or neutral colors together, you'll never end up with a weird combination. These safe color combos can't fail, but they can look a little bit boring. In order to look stylish when coordinating neutral colors, accessorize with a brightly colored bag or shoes.

If your outfits are boring you, buy a brightly colored bag or pair of shoes. And make sure the color is one that wouldn't look out of place in a set of colored pencils. Red or yellow, green or blue, whichever one you prefer.

Pairing masculine clothing like wide-leg pants and denim with brightly colored items can look very refined.

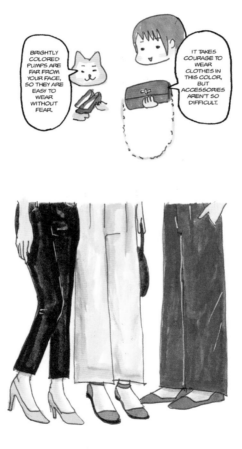

Of course, you might also want to buy a scarf in those colors.

WHEN YOU WEAR A SCARF, PUTTING YOUR HAIR UP IN A SHORT PONYTAIL LOOKS REALLY STYLISH!

ADDING A RED SCARF TO A MONOCHROME OUTFIT— BLACK SKINNY JEANS AND A GRAY LONG CARDIGAN, FOR EXAMPLE—TAKES ABOUT FIVE YEARS OFF YOUR APPEARANCE.

IT'S AMAZING!

WOOL SLIPPERS WILL KEEP YOUR ANKLES WARM EVEN IN THE COLD.

- Gray wool ribbed knit coat
- Thermal black leggings
- Red plaid scarf
- Tan fur-lined slippers
- Black quilted chain purse

Tip #3   I'm messy, but all of my hangers still match.

A real benefit of fast fashion shops is the sheer scope of their stock, right?

MEOW! THERE'S SO MANY!

Even if a shop doesn't have a lot of space, they're able to fit so so much product onto their racks because all of the hangers are exactly the same.

Often, the argument for having matching hangers is that they look better. That's true, of course, but also, using identical hangers can dramatically increase just how much you're able to store at home!

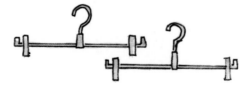

When you look at hangers from the side, you'll see no wasted space if the hooks and the hanging portion are at the same angle. Therefore, in a house with very little storage space, if you own one hanger for each piece of clothing you have, you'll be able to increase the amount of space you have available by up to 30 percent.

I use German Mawa hangers. They're about two dollars apiece, which is pretty expensive, but I haven't broken one in the ten years since I purchased them. You can get nice hangers at the dollar store, of course, but between generic-brand items and something like Mawa, it's smarter to go with an established brand because they'll be easier to find again if you ever need to replace one in the future.

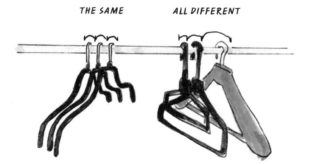

THE SAME   ALL DIFFERENT

30 Choose a pedicure over a manicure.

IN THE EVENINGS DURING SUMMERTIME, I WEAR A BREATHABLE PAJAMA SET. IT'S VERY COMFORTABLE.

THE PAJAMAS ARE MADE OF RAYON, THE TEXTURE IS NICE AND SMOOTH. ♥

- Breathable pajama set

When the summer starts, try getting a pedicure. Once your toenails are painted, you'll be fashionable all summer long. Manicures tend to show wear and tear if you don't take regular care of them, but even if your toes are painted in a messy way, it's hard to notice. Your toenails grow more slowly than your fingernails, and when they do grow, it's very easy just to patch the color up.

Adding color to your toenails—where people don't often check—can look very showy. If you don't want to get a professional pedicure, it's just fine to just paint them yourself.

I have three color recommendations: red, sparkling gold or sparkling silver.

Red makes your feet look healthy and sexy, adding to your charm.

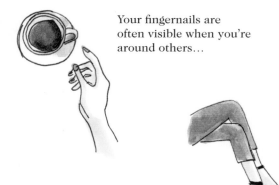

Your fingernails are often visible when you're around others…

…but your toenails are far from their line of sight. Even if you don't touch-up the paint and leave it messy, it's no big deal!

Sparkles are ideal because they obscure imperfections or missed areas. It's so easy to apply yourself—I highly recommend it.

PEDICURES ARE BETTER BECAUSE...
• THEY LAST LONGER,
• IT'S DIFFICULT TO SEE IMPERFECTIONS AND
• THEY'RE EASY TO DO ON YOUR OWN, WHICH MAKES IT EASY TO LEND YOURSELF A HAND!
(OR A FOOT, MEOW!)

IT'S TOUGH TO PAINT YOUR HANDS.

YOU'RE RIGHT!

With a topcoat, your pedicure will last up to two weeks. It's easy to just ignore your toenails and leave them as they are, but just painting them red will make you look so much more fashionable, so please give it a try.

SHOWING SOME SKIN WHEN YOU WEAR A BLACK OUTFIT WILL MAKE YOU LOOK HEALTHY.

RED IS A GREAT COLOR, AS ARE SPARKLY GOLD AND SILVER!

Cool colors can make the tips of your toes look like they have bad circulation.

If you try to do nail art, it will be very small and not be as obvious as if it were on your hands.

THONG SANDALS MAKE YOUR FEET LOOK SLIM AND DAINTY. WHEN YOU WEAR SHOES LIKE THAT, YOU'LL LOOK VERY SOPHISTICATED.

- Black collar dress
- Tan purse

31 Stockings are very convenient.

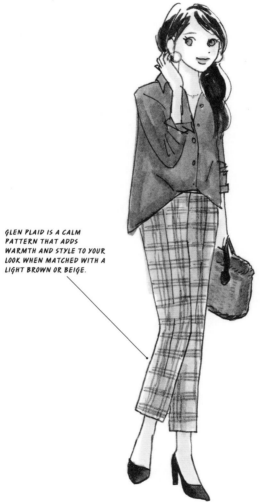

GLEN PLAID IS A CALM
PATTERN THAT ADDS
WARMTH AND STYLE TO YOUR
LOOK WHEN MATCHED WITH A
LIGHT BROWN OR BEIGE.

- Light brown soft cotton shirt
- Glen plaid ankle-length pants
- Black pumps
- Wicker handbag

Sometimes wearing shoes with no socks can chafe your skin. On the other hand, liner socks slip off too easily, don't they?

Stockings protect your feet from chafing and allow you to show off your skin at the same time. They're a great all-purpose item.

They're very easy to wear as long as you pay attention.

Looking effortless and natural—meaning, looking stylish—is possible without worrying too much about minor details. Stockings are a fashionable choice.

As you get older, stockings can help your skin can look smoother and more even.

Next is how to choose your stockings. Pay close attention to these things when purchasing these four items.

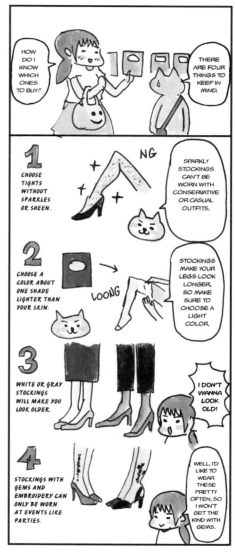

Don't buy stockings in greige (gray and beige). Instead, buy them in brown, which has a little more red to it. That will make your circulation look much better. This chart shows why you should avoid greige stockings and embrace brown ones for healthier-looking legs!

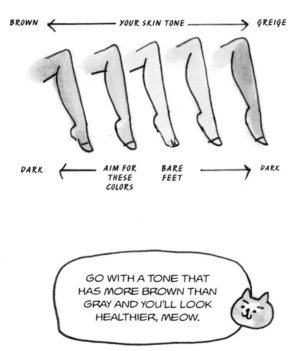

Knee-high stockings are very convenient for wearing with pants.

32 For adults, the best T-shirts are plain, lettered or striped.

WEARING A T-SHIRT WITH NOTHING BUT A BRAND LOGO ON IT MAKES YOU LOOK STYLISH!!

IN THE SUMMER, ONLY WEAR BLACK IF IT'S SLIGHTLY SEE-THROUGH. IT WILL MAKE YOU LOOK NICE AND COOL AND GIVE A REAL BOOST TO YOUR STYLE!

LACE IS ALSO COOLING.

- Black transparent skirt
- Brand label T-shirt
- Black sandals
- Leather handbag

Choosing the wrong kind of T-shirt can make you look older. But if you don't wear T-shirts at all, you can never hope to survive the summer. You can wear them under cardigans and jackets to keep using them all year round. Successfully incorporating T-shirts into your outfits can really make an impression, so here are some tips and tricks to doing it right!

There are three types of T-shirt that you need to make sure you own!

Plain T-shirts

They can be used under jackets and so on too.

DESATURATED COLOR   RIBBED T-SHIRT   THICK T-SHIRT

T-SHIRTS ARE CASUAL ITEMS, SO AVOID WEARING COLORS THAT ARE TOO FLASHY. CALM COLORS SOOTHE THE EYE.

NO GOOD

Lettered T-shirts

Cursive writing makes you look cool!

Shirts with brand logos on them look really cool, so be sure to buy those when you find them.

Striped T-shirts

They are so easy to use. They go with any bottoms you pair them with.

ONES WITH SKINNIER STRIPES LOOK MORE GROWN-UP!

THIS'LL MAKE GETTING THROUGH HOT SUMMERS A SNAP!

WHEW!

NOW I CAN WEAR T-SHIRTS AND STILL LOOK STYLISH!

If you buy heavy-duty shirts in loose sizes, you have a chance to exercise your fashion sense as an adult.

WHEN YOU'RE YOUNG, IT'S FINE TO WEAR FITTED T-SHIRTS.

FOR OLDER WOMEN, IT'S GOOD TO WEAR A NICE HEAVY-DUTY SHIRT THAT HANGS LOOSE.

MY BODY SHAPE ISN'T BEING SHOWN TO EVERYONE, WHICH MAKES ME FEEL LESS ANXIOUS.

RIBBED SHIRTS LOOK CLEAN. THEY PAIR WELL WITH FEMININE OUTFITS.

IT'S COOL, BUT I LOOK PUT TOGETHER TOO! ♥

Here are a few ways to use T-shirts in your wardrobe.

Plain T-shirts

CREW NECK T-SHIRTS!!
THE FABRIC IS NICE
AND THICK, SO IT LOOKS
EXPENSIVE. THEY ALSO COME
IN MANY DIFFERENT COLORS.

PASTEL SHIRTS CAN
BE PAIRED WITH
EARRINGS FOR
A LITTLE EXTRA
BRIGHTNESS.

I RECOMMEND
WEARING THEM
UNDER A JACKET.

- Crew neck T-shirt
- High-waisted wide pants
- Blue sandals
- Black accent woven bag

Striped T-shirt

NAVY BLUE STRIPES ARE VERY POPULAR. YOU MAY END UP WEARING THE SAME SHIRT AS SOMEONE ELSE. THAT'S WHY I RECOMMEND BLACK STRIPES.

SHIRTS WITH A MORE OPEN NECKLINE OR THAT ARE MADE OF A RIBBED FABRIC LOOK MORE FEMININE, SO I RECOMMEND WEARING THEM WITH A SKIRT. ❤

- Black striped T-shirt
- Skirt
- Pointed flat shoes

33 Try to wear something white in the summertime.

PUTTING YOUR HAIR UP IN THE SUMMER KEEPS YOU COOL AND LOOKS VERY STYLISH. TWO BIRDS WITH ONE STONE!

THIS OUTFIT INCORPORATES A WHITE WOVEN BAG AND WHITE SNEAKERS. THESE TWO ITEMS WORK INCREDIBLY WELL FOR SUMMER OUTFITS! IF YOU WEAR THEM TOGETHER, YOU LOOK REALLY VIBRANT!!

- Navy V-neck T-shirt
- High-waisted tan chinos
- White lace tank top
- White canvas sneakers
- White woven bag

It's very simple to look fashionable during the hot, hot summer. Make sure to wear something white in your outfit.

Just by adding one white item, you'll suddenly look more vibrant and feel cooler.

Even the influence of small accessories like earrings and bracelets is enough to give you a summer vibe.

Just wear one thing in white and choose what you want for the rest of the outfit. It's a very simple way to create a look!

Here are a few white items that are worth investing in:

SWITCH FROM A REGULAR STRAW HAT TO A WHITE HAT.

WEAR A TRANSPARENT OR WHITE BRACELET.

WEAR A WHITE SUN-PROTECTIVE CARDIGAN OVER A LITTLE BLACK DRESS.

A BANDANA!

SANDALS!

A CLUTCH BAG!

WEAR WHITE SNEAKERS WITH YOUR WIDE-LEG PANTS.

TRY CLEAR GLASS OR SHELL EARRINGS.

LET A WHITE TANK TOP PEEK OUT OF YOUR TOP.

WEAR WHITE ANKLE-LENGTH PANTS AT THE OFFICE FOR A SUPREMELY CLEAN LOOK!

There are many more options to choose from!

Try many different white bags.

MAISON KITSUNÉ PARIS FRANCE

Or a belt!

Linen shirt

Skirt

34

Wearing a long cardigan in the summer kills three birds with one stone.

WEARING A SLEEVELESS SWEATER WITH SUN-PROTECTIVE FEATURES AND A CARDIGAN WILL MAKE YOU LOOK FASHIONABLE AND PROTECT YOU FROM SUNBURN.

A LEATHER BAG WITH A BAMBOO HANDLE IS VERY USEFUL. IT GIVES YOU A HIGH-CLASS, SOPHISTICATED VIBE, SO IF YOU FIND ONE, CONSIDER YOURSELF LUCKY.

IF YOU'RE WEARING AN ALL-WHITE OUTFIT, MAKE SURE THE TOP AND BOTTOM ARE MADE OF DIFFERENT MATERIALS. IT GIVES OFF A GOOD FEELING.

- Sun-protective gray dolman long-sleeve cardigan
- Sun-protective white ribbed sleeveless sweater
- Loose white ankle-length pants
- Black sandals

From the end of spring to the beginning of fall, I recommend a long cardigan for chilly days. A long cardigan is something that no woman should be without.

Thin-knitted cardigans in particular give a very feminine air. They're an all-purpose item for making you look sophisticated and dignified no matter what they're worn over.

WHEN YOU'RE WEARING A LONG CARDIGAN IN A PALE COLOR, A BLACK DRESS CAN REALLY TIE THE WHOLE THING TOGETHER.

WEARING A LONG CARDIGAN WITH LONG PANTS CAN GIVE PEOPLE THE IMPRESSION THAT YOU'RE HEAVIER THAN YOU ACTUALLY ARE, SO PAIR THEM WITH A V-NECK OR SOME DELICATE SANDALS TO SHOW OFF YOUR SKIN A BIT MORE.

- White linen-blend cardigan
- Brown strappy sandals
- White tote

- White linen-blend cardigan
- Black dress
- Yellow sandals
- Macrame bag

35 Make sure your winter outerwear is navy blue.

WEARING A FUR-LINED HOOD CALLS ATTENTION TO YOUR FACE AND MAKES YOU LOOK OUTSTANDING EVEN WITHOUT ANY ACCESSORIES.

WEARING OFF-WHITE IN THE WINTER MAKES YOU LOOK GRACEFUL.

TUCKING YOUR PANTS INTO YOUR BOOTS MAKES YOUR LEGS LOOK LONG AND TAPERED. IT'S AMAZING!!

A down jacket is absolutely the most difficult to look stylish in. But once you've learned how to wear it well, it's easy.

- Light-blue cashmere V-neck sweater
- White thermal leggings
- Brown boots
- Black bamboo-handle tote

The trick to wearing down coats well is to not buy them in black! That's it.

When it comes to buying a down coat, navy is my best recommendation.

Black is such a heavy color that you can get buried in it as you get older...

If you're thinking about buying coats in black, just choose navy instead. It's got a little bit of brightness to it, and it can make even a down jacket work with feminine outfits.

There are a few points to consider when choosing a down jacket, including making sure that the design of the jacket isn't too casual. Ignoring this advice will lead directly to buying a jacket that's entirely too casual.

Look at this coat, which ignores these points. It's shapeless and out of style.

A shorter-length down coat looks good with a more feminine outfit.

YOU CAN PUT A SHORT COAT ON QUICKLY. WITH A BELT ATTACHED, IT GIVES YOU A SLIM LOOK.

A KNIT-SWEATER-AND-SKIRT SET MADE WITH THE SAME MATERIAL GIVES YOU A FEMININE, SEXY AIR. ♡ ♡

STUDS MAKE BLACK SHOES LOOK LESS HEAVY.

- Lamb's wool V-neck sweater
- Merino-blend ribbed skirt
- Black studded shoes
- Leather handbag

36 Buy wool coats in beige or gray.

A COLLARLESS COAT WITH A SCARF OR TURTLENECK MEANS EVEN YOUR NECK WILL LOOK COOL.

YOU CAN PUT THE ENDS OF YOUR BELT IN YOUR POCKET WHEN IT'S NOT TIED.

WEARING SHOES AND TIGHTS IN DIFFERENT COLORS LOOKS QUITE FASHIONABLE IN THE WINTER.

- Beige wool coat
- Black sweater
- Black pumps
- Black leather tote bag

There's one more type of coat that it's important to own—a wool coat in a neutral color. With this one item, you're covered for fancier, more formal situations when a down jacket just won't do.

Beige and gray are neutral colors, so they'll go well with any other colors you put them with. Also, wearing neutral colors in the wintertime is stylish in and of itself.

EVEN IF YOU'RE WEARING THE COAT OVER BLACK, YOU WON'T LOOK TOO INTENSE.

CHECKED OR PLAID ACCESSORIES GO PERFECTLY WITH IT, TOO!

Give it a try yourself.

37 Buy your scarves in bright colors.

Even if you do decide to get a black coat, make sure to at least put something colorful on your neck.

Try to buy a scarf or a stole in a nice bright color.

If the area around your face is bright, the impression of your entire outfit gets a little brighter too.

You can look so much brighter just by wearing a colored scarf!!

ALWAYS WEAR A SCARF WHEN ALL YOUR OUTERWEAR IS A DARK COLOR.

A VOLUMINOUS SCARF MAKES YOUR FACE LOOK MUCH SMALLER.

WHEN YOU WEAR YOUR HAIR DOWN, WEARING IT INSIDE THE SCARF LOOKS MUCH MORE STYLISH.

IF YOU PULL YOUR HAIR OUT WHEN YOU PUT ON YOUR SCARF, IT MAKES YOUR FACE LOOK MUCH LARGER AND WIDER.

DUN DUN

38 Don't buy thermal wear in black.

IF YOU LIKE WEARING TIGHT SHIRTS, WEARING A PINK THERMAL CAMISOLE OR ONE THAT'S CLOSE TO YOUR SKIN TONE WILL KEEP YOUR TOP FROM BEING SEE-THROUGH.

SUPIMA COTTON STRETCH SHIRTS DON'T WRINKLE, SO HAVING ONE AROUND IS REALLY CONVENIENT!!

A SMALL CHECKED PATTERN CAN BE USED WITH FEMININE OUTFITS, AND SINCE THAT CAN ACT AS THE STAR OF THE OUTFIT, IT MAKES PICKING THE REST OF YOUR CLOTHING EASIER!!

A WRAP SKIRT COVERS THE ENTIRETY OF THE BELLY AREA FOR YOU.

- White Supima cotton stretch shirt
- Checked pencil skirt
- Brown pumps

If you sport thermal wear, sometimes it's visible under your clothes. I can't even guess how people manage to wear it without ever letting it show. But I'm going to give you tips on how to use thermal wear so that it doesn't really matter if people can see it!

The most popular thermal wear almost always come in black.

But even when you're just showing a bit of black, it really stands out!

Try to buy thermal under-clothes in a light gray.

When people glimpse gray clothing under someone's clothes, they don't imme-diately assume that it's underwear.

If you want to buy colors other than gray, try pink instead, or another color suited to your skin tone.

Here are some more recommendations for looking great in thermal wear:

When you're in short sleeves…

SHORT-SLEEVED SWEATER

U-NECK THERMAL T-SHIRT

A SHORT-SLEEVED SHIRT CAN BE WORN UNTIL THE BEGINNING OF SPRING.

When you have an open collar…

OPEN-COLLARED TOPS

THERMAL BALLET-NECK TOP WITH 3/4 SLEEVES.

THIS IS THE MOST OPEN-COLLARED OF THE THERMAL SHIRTS YOU CAN FIND.

When you're outside and it's cold…

GO!

…LIKE WHEN YOU'RE AT A SPORTING EVENT…

ULTRAWARM THERMAL CREW NECK T-SHIRT WITH LONG SLEEVES

THIS IS 2.25 TIMES WARMER THAN A NORMAL THERMAL SHIRT.

When at a party or another event where you must wear clothing that is thin, this is how you do it.

THERMAL TANK TOP WITH BRA

PUT HEAT PADS ON YOUR BELLY AND BACK.

THERMAL U-NECK T-SHIRT WITH SHORT SLEEVES

THERMAL SHORTS

PUT HEAT PADS IN THE TIPS OF YOUR SHOES.

THIS WAY, YOU CAN BE WARM WITHOUT ANYONE REALIZING.

If you wear a bra tank top under another thermal item, you'll feel very warm, even if you are wearing short sleeves.

When you add in heat pads to warm up your stomach, you can look put together and fashionable without sacrificing yourself to the cold.

When you want to go back to wearing thin clothes, you can try wearing a camisole over your thermal wear. Try a camisole with lace! Lace camisoles don't look like underwear, so having a few is really useful.

39

You don't need to be tough to wear skirts in the winter, if you layer your thermal wear.

A MOTORCYCLE JACKET, EVEN ONE MADE OF SYNTHETIC MATERIALS, BLOCKS THE WIND, KEEPING YOU NICE AND WARM.

IF YOU MATCH A FULL SKIRT WITH A SHORT OUTER JACKET, YOU WILL GET A VERY FEMININE SILHOUETTE.

BEING ABLE TO CARRY SUPER-CUTE FLUFFY PURSES IS ONE OF THE BEST THINGS ABOUT WINTER. ♡

- Faux leather motorcycle jacket
- Gray scarf
- Black boots
- Fake fur bag

Sometimes you just really want to wear a skirt, even if it's the middle of the winter. On those days, I recommend wearing thermals underneath it. Using both thermal tights and shorts will keep your belly really warm!

40 Down jacket liners broaden the scope of fashion in the wintertime.

A DOWN JACKET LINER EXPANDS THE SCOPE OF YOUR WINTER OUTFITS DRAMATICALLY!!

IT'LL REVOLUTIONIZE YOUR OUTERWEAR FASHION WORLD!

WEARING MANY LAYERS MAKES STATIC ELECTRICITY REALLY BAD, SO PICK UP SOME STATIC CLING SPRAY. IT'S REALLY CONVENIENT, MEOW.

- Light-blue knit dress
- Ultralight down compact coat
- Black pumps

If you want to wear a down coat but it won't go well with the outfit you're wearing, that's when you really should wear a light down jacket instead.

If you can buy only one, the jacket style is the most useful.

Wearing a thick sweater or wool pants can make you look like you're wearing too many layers, which is unfashionable. A down jacket is much more convenient.

In the spring, when it's too warm to wear a full coat, wearing a down jacket under a hoodie can keep you nice and warm as well.

YOU CAN EVEN FIND ULTRALIGHT DOWN JACKETS THAT COMPRESS INTO A BAG SMALL ENOUGH TO FIT IN YOUR POCKET.

WEAR IT UNDER A HOODIE OR A DENIM JACKET.

I also recommend a down jacket for times when the air conditioning is too cold. It's not so heavy on your shoulders and it won't pill, so it's very convenient.

You can buy light down jackets for low prices. They're warm, light and compact enough to keep handy without giving up a lot of space. They're very convenient to have around.

41 Pair your military outerwear with cute items.

MAKE SURE YOU CHOOSE A JACKET THAT IS IN YOUR SIZE!! IF IT'S TOO LARGE, THE TOUGH VIBE OF THE JACKET MAY DOMINATE YOUR OUTFIT.

AN MA-1 BOMBER JACKET PAIRS INCREDIBLY WELL WITH A TULLE SKIRT!!

IF THE REST OF THE OUTFIT IS MONOCHROME, YOU'LL END UP WITH A CUTE OUTFIT, BUT ONE THAT'S STILL PRETTY COOL AS WELL.

- MA-1 bomber jacket
- Gray tulle skirt
- Black pumps

It's easy to wear military-style clothing and still look cute. Wear it with lace, pink, frills or anything else cute that you happen to have.

TRY A LACY SLEEVELESS T-SHIRT. A CALM PINK COLOR LOOKS GOOD ON EVERYONE, REGARDLESS OF AGE.

IT'S CUTE TO ROLL UP THE SLEEVES OF YOUR MILITARY JACKET ♡

IF YOU WANT TO WEAR BLACK SNEAKERS, TRY GETTING ONES WITH WHITE LINES!! THOSE KINDS OF SHOES ARE EASY TO MATCH WITH A MORE FEMININE OUTFIT.

- Military jacket
- Pink lace sleeveless T-shirt
- Black-and-white sneakers
- Long-handled waffle-pattern tote

42 Having vision problems gives you an excuse to wear cute glasses.

WHEN YOU WEAR GLASSES, TYING YOUR HAIR UP IN A LOOSE WAY WILL GIVE YOU A SOFTER APPEARANCE.

A WICKER BAG WITH LEATHER ELEMENTS CAN BE USED ALL YEAR ROUND.

PAIRING WIDE-LEGGED PANTS WITH SHOES THAT BARE YOUR INSTEP WILL MAKE YOUR LEGS LOOK LONG AND THIN.

PUTTING A FUR OR SCARF ON THE PURSE WILL ADD A SEASONAL FEELING AND MAKE YOUR LOOK MORE BEAUTIFUL. ♡

- Glasses
- Yellow overalls
- Shiny ribbed frill-necked sweater
- Brown flats
- Plaid scarf

As you reach the age of 40, your eyesight changes and you become less able to see small characters. Yes, the effects of presbyopia!

It's a road we'll all have to walk down at some point. Rather than dreading it, let's think of it as a chance to wear cute eyeglasses!

Glasses give you a dignified air. There are many designs to choose from, so have fun.

If possible, I recommend wearing glasses with round lenses. They look feminine and match well with cute clothing and casual styles alike. If you want to wear square lenses, get them in silver and make sure the frames are thin. That will make them look a little less stiff.

CHUNKY BLACK GLASSES AND SHORT BLACK HAIR ARE VERY ON TREND.

When choosing your black-frame glasses, be sure not to make them too thick. If the frames are very thick, it can make you look a little childish.

Tortoiseshell frames make your profile look very cool. If you're not sure, just know that you can never go wrong with brown tortoiseshell frames.

BROWN TORTOISESHELL
FRAMES ARE EXTREMELY
POWERFUL WHEN PAIRED
WITH A LOOSE HAIRSTYLE.

Thin gold or silver frames make your face look brighter. You won't need any accessories with this one.

SINCE GLASSES PRESENT
SUCH A DIGNIFIED IMAGE YOU
CAN EVEN WEAR YOUR SHIRT
IN A FASHIONABLY CASUAL
WAY WITH THEM.

Tip #4 If you're careful with how you wash your clothes, they'll never get wrinkled.

It's such a pain to iron your clothes! In an effort to do it as infrequently as possible, I've adopted this solution.

The most important part comes when you're drying your clothes. The easiest way to get rid of wrinkles is by patting them with your hands to remove them, and when the article of clothing is dry, putting it in your closet on the same hanger you used to pat it.

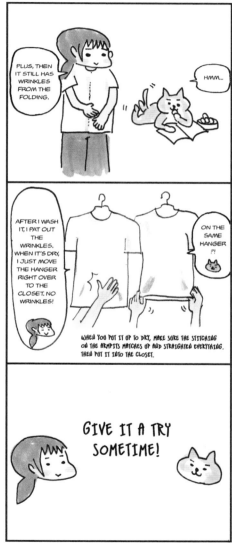

PLUS, THEN IT STILL HAS WRINKLES FROM THE FOLDING.

HMM...

AFTER I WASH IT, I PAT OUT THE WRINKLES. WHEN IT'S DRY, I JUST MOVE THE HANGER RIGHT OVER TO THE CLOSET. NO WRINKLES!

ON THE SAME HANGER ?!

WHEN YOU PUT IT UP TO DRY, MAKE SURE THE STITCHING ON THE ARMPITS MATCHES UP AND STRAIGHTEN EVERYTHING. THEN PUT IT INTO THE CLOSET.

GIVE IT A TRY SOMETIME!

43 Make fashion choices that suit the shape of your face.

What look suits you better?
Casual? Pretty?

Women's faces can be split into two groups: cute and classic. Classic people should wear more feminine and formal fashion, while cute people look better in casual fashion.

Especially once you're over 30, knowing what suits you is one of the most important tricks to being fashionable.

Next, we're going to figure out how to decide if an outfit matches your face type.

For example, here's each of these face types with a flannel-shirt outfit.

Classic

FOR A CLASSIC FACE, FASTENING ALL THE BUTTONS CAN MAKE YOU LOOK A LITTLE TOO STIFF, SO LEAVE A FEW OPEN.

Cute

IF YOUR FACE IS CUTE, THE PLAID PATTERN WORKS, BUT IF YOUR FACE IS CLASSIC, IT'S BETTER TO HAVE NO PATTERN.

A FLANNEL SHIRT IS MADE WITH A MATERIAL THAT IS VERY WARM. I RECOMMEND IT FOR WINTER.

- Gray flannel shirt
- Black pinstripe ankle-length pants
- Tan pumps

- Plaid flannel shirt
- Black wool-blend flare skirt
- White faux fur purse

Here's an outfit built around a jacket.

Classic

FOR A WOMAN WITH A CLASSIC FACE, A TAILORED JACKET AND PANTS LOOK COOL AND SHARP.

Cute

WOMEN WITH CUTE FACES SHOULDN'T WEAR STIFF JACKETS. INSTEAD, TRY COLLARLESS JACKETS OR ONES WITH SHORT HEMS.

- Stretch tailored jacket
- Stretch tailored pants
- Large white bag

- Dark-colored collarless jacket
- Pink stretch cropped pants
- Large silver bag

44

When coordinating your family's outfits, choose one matching color.

CHILDREN HAVE TROUBLE WEARING LEATHER SHOES, SO TRY BLACK SNEAKERS OR, FOR A MORE FEMININE TOUCH, BALLET SHOES.

The key to making matched outfits look effortless is to focus on one color. As long as you're all wearing the same color, it doesn't matter if everyone's patterns or designs are different. Trying to match materials and designs makes it harder to find clothing and can look a little overbearing.

Navy and black are the easiest colors to match with in a coordinated family outfit.

It's pretty cute when kids wear adult-style clothes. It creates a little dissonance between their outfit and their age.

WHEN YOU HAVE SMALL CHILDREN, IT'S BEST THAT THEY WEAR SLIP-ONS OR OTHER SHOES THAT ARE EASY TO TAKE ON AND OFF.

Papa
- Black extrafine merino crew neck sweater
- Stretch selvedge denim slim-fit jeans

Mama
- Black sweater
- Tan cotton circular skirt
- Canvas sneakers
- Green backpack

Child
- Ultrastretch denim easy-on pants
- Black sweatshirt
- Black sneakers

If you match the outfits of the adults and the kids too closely, the adults are going to look embarrassingly young.

Matching small parts of your outfit gives you a cute matched outfit set without drawing too much attention to it. To accomplish this, make sure to choose simple items!

DIFFERENT SNEAKERS FROM
THE SAME BRAND

YOU'RE DOING IT RIGHT WHEN
OTHER PEOPLE THINK, "IF YOU
LOOK CLOSELY AT THEM, THEY
MATCH!" AND THEN FEEL
PLEASED WITH THEMSELVES
FOR NOTICING.

GLASSES MADE BY
THE SAME BRAND

Part 2

FOR MEN

KEEP YOUR
BOTTOMS BLACK,
NAVY OR GRAY.

*It's pretty easy to look fashionable
if you're a man.*

45 Don't wear shirts with large checks if you're a man over 30.

I RECOMMEND EXTRAFINE COTTON SHIRTS. THE FABRIC IS THIN AND YOU CAN USE THEM IN BOTH CASUAL AND PROFESSIONAL SETTINGS. →

WHEN YOU GET TO BE OVER 30, I RECOMMEND MATCHING YOUR SHIRTS WITH SWEATERS INSTEAD OF SWEATSHIRTS.

UNWASHED OR RAW DENIM IS DARK, WHICH MAKES MEN LOOK QUITE DIGNIFIED AND COOL.

- Extrafine merino V-neck sweater
- Extrafine cotton plaid shirt
- Stretch selvedge denim fitted jeans

I'm sorry, but I have to ban men from wearing large patterned plaid shirts.

It's an item many men wear while they're in college, but when older men wear it, they tend to look really awkward.

Now I'd like to talk about a few items that make adult men look much more refined and cool.

SHIRTS WITH SMALL PLAID PATTERNS, STRIPES OR NO PATTERN AT ALL ARE BEST.

UNDERNEATH THE SHIRT, A MOCK TURTLENECK T-SHIRT KEEPS YOU WARM AND LOOKS FASHIONABLE.

WHEN THINGS GET COLDER AND YOU NEED TO LAYER TO STAY WARM, IT'S VERY EASY TO COORDINATE OUTFITS WITH SIMPLE PATTERNLESS SHIRTS.

A GRAY STRIPED SHIRT WITH A BROWN SWEATER COMBINES WINTER COLORS. THIS IS AN EASY OUTFIT FOR MEN.

If you keep your shirts simple, they'll match whatever bottoms you wear, including jeans, slacks and even chinos. Definitely try to buy thin fabrics, though.

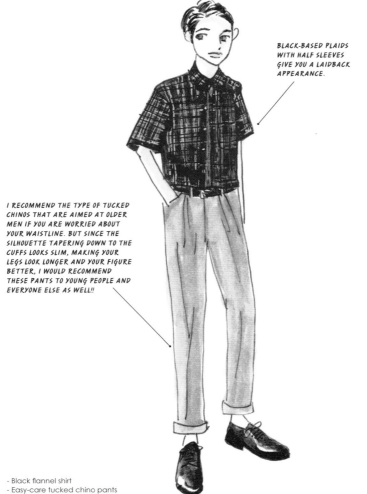

BLACK-BASED PLAIDS WITH HALF SLEEVES GIVE YOU A LAIDBACK APPEARANCE.

I RECOMMEND THE TYPE OF TUCKED CHINOS THAT ARE AIMED AT OLDER MEN IF YOU ARE WORRIED ABOUT YOUR WAISTLINE. BUT SINCE THE SILHOUETTE TAPERING DOWN TO THE CUFFS LOOKS SLIM, MAKING YOUR LEGS LOOK LONGER AND YOUR FIGURE BETTER, I WOULD RECOMMEND THESE PANTS TO YOUNG PEOPLE AND EVERYONE ELSE AS WELL!!

- Black flannel shirt
- Easy-care tucked chino pants
- Black dress shoes

46 There's nothing wrong with men wearing high-water pants.

IF YOU'RE COLD, YOU CAN WEAR A DOWN JACKET LINER INSTEAD OF A CARDIGAN UNDER YOUR JACKET. IT LOOKS SUPER COOL AND I HIGHLY RECOMMEND IT! OBVIOUSLY, IT'LL KEEP YOU WARM, AND AS LONG AS IT'S A V-NECK IT WON'T BE TOO OBVIOUS TO OTHER PEOPLE. PLUS, IT'S LIGHT AND IT WON'T PILL UP!

ANKLE-LENGTH PANTS IN A WOOL-LIKE FABRIC ARE EASY TO WEAR IN THE OFFICE AND PROVIDE A SHARP SILHOUETTE.

- Wool-blend comfort jacket
- Black ankle-length slacks
- Ultralight down compact vest
- Black business shoes

For men, shorter pants are the most fashionable.

Your legs will look longer in them. Though it's best to have them hemmed, if you think that's too much work or someone else buys clothes for you, buying ankle-length pants to begin with is your best bet.

Slacks like these won't need any hemming to be ankle length.

These pants look sharp enough that you can even wear them to work. You can buy them in wool for warmth in the winter.

They're fairly narrow below the knee, which means that no matter your body shape, your legs will look slimmer and longer in them.

Compared to other types of jeans, you can wear these without having to hem them. Some of them also have drawstrings, so they can be worn easily by people who don't like belts. The material is soft, so wearing them is really comfortable.

A STURDY BACKPACK AND HIGH-TECH SNEAKERS ARE UNREFINED ITEMS THAT MAKE YOU LOOK MANLY AND COOL.

REGARDING THE ANKLE-LENGTH JEANS I MENTIONED, THE FABRIC IS VERY SOFT AND STRETCHY, SO PEOPLE WHO AREN'T USED TO FEELING CONSTRAINED IN SKINNY JEANS CAN WEAR THEM WITHOUT STRESSING OUT.

- Cotton hoodie
- Ankle-length jeans
- Sports sneakers
- Backpack

47 Make your bottoms black, navy or gray.

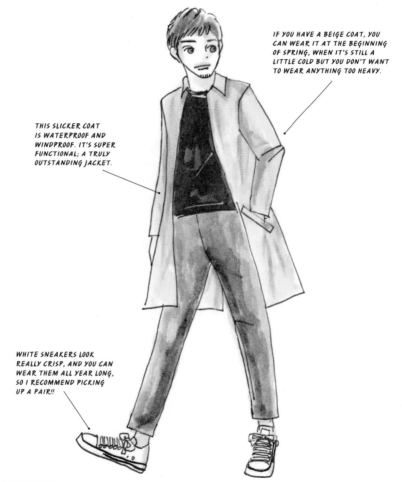

IF YOU HAVE A BEIGE COAT, YOU CAN WEAR IT AT THE BEGINNING OF SPRING, WHEN IT'S STILL A LITTLE COLD BUT YOU DON'T WANT TO WEAR ANYTHING TOO HEAVY.

THIS SLICKER COAT IS WATERPROOF AND WINDPROOF. IT'S SUPER FUNCTIONAL; A TRULY OUTSTANDING JACKET.

WHITE SNEAKERS LOOK REALLY CRISP, AND YOU CAN WEAR THEM ALL YEAR LONG, SO I RECOMMEND PICKING UP A PAIR!!

- Beige slicker coat
- Cashmere crew neck sweater
- Gray ankle-length jeans
- White canvas sneakers

For men, getting your pants in black, navy or gray will never fail.

These are the three colors most often used in men's suits.

Just as there is no man who doesn't look good in a suit, there's no man who doesn't look good in these three colors of pants.

Here's our next outfit example.

Wearing a black top with a blue bottom makes you look intellectual and cool!

WHEN WEARING A T-SHIRT AS AN ADULT, YOU WANT TO CHOOSE ONE THAT IS MADE OF THICK FABRIC. THAT SMALL DETAIL MAKES IT MUCH LESS LIKELY TO LOOK LIKE AN UNDERSHIRT.

WHEN WEARING T-SHIRTS, IT'S EXTRA COOL TO WEAR LEATHER DRESS SHOES.

- Black crew neck T-shirt
- Navy ankle-length pants
- Black dress shoes

A white shirt with black pants is the most basic of basic outfits, and it's also incredibly popular.

A WHITE SHIRT WITH BLACK SKINNY JEANS IS REALLY GOOD.

THE SIMPLER YOUR CLOTHING ITEMS ARE, THE MORE YOU'LL WANT TO SPEND ON YOUR ACCESSORIES. IF YOU CAN, TRY TO SPEND AROUND TEN DOLLARS FOR EACH YEAR OF YOUR LIFE ON A NICE SET OF ACCESSORIES, SO YOU PURCHASE NICER THINGS AS YOU GROW OLDER. IF YOU GO WITH THAT AS A GENERAL RULE, YOU'LL BE SURE TO LOOK VERY COOL.

- Slim-fit white shirt
- Black ankle-length pants
- Casual athletic shoes

48 My tip for men's fashion is the smaller, the better.

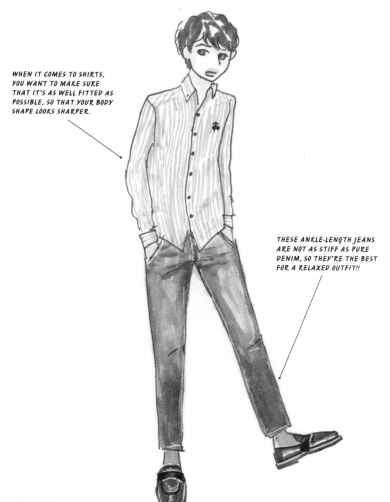

WHEN IT COMES TO SHIRTS, YOU WANT TO MAKE SURE THAT IT'S AS WELL FITTED AS POSSIBLE, SO THAT YOUR BODY SHAPE LOOKS SHARPER.

THESE ANKLE-LENGTH JEANS ARE NOT AS STIFF AS PURE DENIM, SO THEY'RE THE BEST FOR A RELAXED OUTFIT!!

- Blue striped shirt
- Gray ankle-length jeans
- Black loafers

My best tip for men's fashion is much the same as my tip for women's fashion—the smaller a logo is, for instance, the more fashionable it will seem.

The most fashionable approach is to wear clothing that makes people casually go, "Now that I look closer, that's a brand logo!" or "Now that I'm paying attention, that's a cartoon character!"

The hurdle for wearing clothes that express your individuality is a lot higher for men than for women. This is because the clothing that is more expressive for men is harder to wear without it looking awkward. It takes study and experience to master.

Wearing a knit top with a pair of chinos gives you a refined appearance that feels classic but is still very modern. An effortless feel is very popular these days!

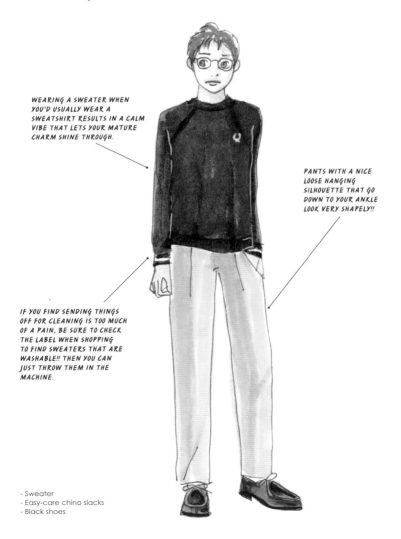

WEARING A SWEATER WHEN YOU'D USUALLY WEAR A SWEATSHIRT RESULTS IN A CALM VIBE THAT LETS YOUR MATURE CHARM SHINE THROUGH.

PANTS WITH A NICE LOOSE HANGING SILHOUETTE THAT GO DOWN TO YOUR ANKLE LOOK VERY SHAPELY!!

IF YOU FIND SENDING THINGS OFF FOR CLEANING IS TOO MUCH OF A PAIN, BE SURE TO CHECK THE LABEL WHEN SHOPPING TO FIND SWEATERS THAT ARE WASHABLE!! THEN YOU CAN JUST THROW THEM IN THE MACHINE.

- Sweater
- Easy-care chino slacks
- Black shoes

The items illustrated in this book are all
items I personally own. In some cases,
these items will no longer be available.
Please be understanding if this is the case.

TOKYO FASHION
A COMIC BOOK

VIZ MEDIA Edition
BY NODOKA

Translation: Abby Lehrke
Retouch & Lettering: Evan Waldinger
Design: Yukiko Whitley
Editor: David Brothers

Published by VIZ Media, LLC
P.O. Box 77010
San Francisco, CA 94107

10 9 8 7 6 5 4 3 2 1
First Printing, March 2021

VIZ MEDIA

viz.com